RAYMOND JACK TYLER

CAIQUES AS PETS

First published by Raymond Jack Tyler 2024

Copyright © 2024 by Raymond Jack Tyler

All rights reserved. No part of this publication may be reproduced, stored or transmitted in any form or by any means, electronic, mechanical, photocopying, recording, scanning, or otherwise without written permission from the publisher. It is illegal to copy this book, post it to a website, or distribute it by any other means without permission.

First edition

This book was professionally typeset on Reedsy. Find out more at reedsy.com

Contents

- 1 **Chapter 1** — 1
  - INTRODUCTION TO CAIQUES — 1
    - Overview Of Caiques — 2
    - History And Origin — 3
    - Different Types Of Caiques — 5
    - Why Caiques Make Great Pets — 7
    - Understanding Caique Temperament — 8
  - CHOOSING THE RIGHT CAIQUE — 10
    - What To Look For In A Healthy Caique — 10
    - Adopting From Breeders Vs. Rescues — 12
    - Male Vs. Female Caiques — 14
    - Caique Age And Lifespan — 16
    - Preparing Your Home For A Caique — 17
- 2 **Chapter 2** — 20
  - SETTING UP THE PERFECT HABITAT — 20
    - Cage Size And Bar Spacing Requirements — 20
    - Cage Location And Environment — 22
    - Perches And Cage Furnishings — 24
    - Toys And Enrichment Items — 26
    - Cleaning And Maintenance Of The Habitat — 28
  - NUTRITION AND DIET — 29
    - Basic Dietary Needs Of Caiques — 29
    - Fresh Fruits And Vegetables — 31
    - Seeds, Nuts, And Pellets: What's Best? — 33
    - Foods To Avoid — 34
    - Establishing A Feeding Routine — 36

3 Chapter 3 — 39
HEALTH AND WELLNESS — 39
- Common Health Issues In Caiques — 39
- Signs Of Illness And When To Call A Vet — 41
- Parasites And Disease Prevention — 43
- Grooming And Bathing Your Caique — 44
- First Aid For Your Parrot — 46

BONDING WITH YOUR CAIQUE — 48
- Building Trust And Rapport — 48
- Understanding Caique Body Language — 50
- The Importance Of Social Interaction — 52
- How To Handle A Shy Or Fearful Caique — 53
- Bonding Activities For Parrot And Owner — 55

4 Chapter 4 — 58
BASIC TRAINING TECHNIQUES — 58
- Positive Reinforcement Training — 58
- Teaching Step-Up And Step-Down Commands — 60
- Training Your Caique To Come When Called — 62
- Training: What It Is Target And How To Use It — 63
- Handling Nipping And Biting Behavior — 65

ADVANCED TRAINING AND TRICKS — 66
- Teaching Your Caique To Talk — 67
- How To Train Fun Tricks (Flips, And Spins) — 69
- Clicker Training For Caiques — 71
- Problem Solving With Trick Training — 73
- Managing Training Expectations — 75

5 Chapter 5 — 77
PLAYTIME AND ENRICHMENT — 77
- Importance Of Mental Stimulation For Caiques — 77
- Creating A Daily Play Routine — 79
- DIY Toys And Activities — 81
- Foraging Games And Puzzle Feeders — 83
- Interactive Play With Your Caique — 85

UNDERSTANDING CAIQUE BEHAVIOR 87
  Exploring The Playful Nature Of Caiques 87
  Aggression And Hormonal Changes 89
  Vocalization: Chirps, Whistles, And Calls 92
  Caique Quirks And Unique Behaviors 94
  How To Deal With Behavioral Challenges 96

6 Chapter 6 99
SOCIALIZING YOUR CAIQUE 99
  Introducing Your Caique To Other Pets 99
  How Caiques Interact With Other Birds 101
  Managing Multi-Pet Households 103
  Caiques And Children Establishing Safe Boundaries 104
  Taking Your Caique Out In Public 106
TRAVEL AND TRANSPORT 108
  Traveling With Your Caique: Preparation And Tips 108
  Best Travel Cages And Carriers 110
  Reducing Stress During Travel 112
  Vacation And Boarding Options For Caiques 115
  Taking Your Caique On Outdoor Adventures 117

7 Chapter 7 120
BREEDING AND REPRODUCTION 120
  Is Breeding Right For You? 120
  Creating A Suitable Nesting Environment 122
  Breeding Behavior And Mating Rituals 125
  Caring For Eggs And Chicks 127
  Ethical Considerations And Responsibilities 129
CAIQUE LIFESPAN AND AGING 131
  The Stages Of A Caique's Life 131
  Signs Of Aging In Caiques 134
  Adjusting Care For Senior Caiques 135
  Common Health Issues In Older Caiques 137
  Providing Comfort For An Aging Parrot 138

8 Chapter 8 141

CAIQUE SAFETY AND HAZARDS	141
Common Household Dangers (Toxins, And Wires)	141
Pet-Proofing Your Home	143
Handling Emergencies And Accidents	145
Predators And Outdoor Safety	147
Seasonal Safety Tips (Winter, Summer Hazards)	149
EMOTIONAL WELL-BEING OF YOUR CAIQUE	150
Preventing Boredom And Loneliness	150
Managing Stress And Anxiety	152
Dealing With Separation Anxiety	154
Creating A Positive Living Environment	156
Recognizing Emotional Changes In Your Caique	159

1

Chapter 1

INTRODUCTION TO CAIQUES

Caiques are one of the most delightful and unique parrots. Known for their bright colors, playful behavior, and high energy, these small- to medium-sized birds are becoming popular pets around the world. While they might not be as famous as larger parrots like macaws or cockatoos, caiques have gained a loyal fan base thanks to their friendly nature, intelligence, and fun personality.

These birds stand out with their beautiful, colorful feathers. Caiques come in two main types: the black-headed caique and the white-bellied caique. Both types are known for their stunning colors, including shades of green, yellow, orange, and white. Their bright appearance, combined with their energetic behavior, makes them hard to miss.

One of the main reasons people love caiques is because of how playful they are. They love to climb, hop, and explore their surroundings, and they are often described as little clowns due to their silly antics. Caiques enjoy playing with toys and interacting with their owners. Unlike some parrots that might sit quietly in a cage, caiques are always on the move and full of energy.

Caiques are also known for their affectionate nature. They form strong bonds with their owners and enjoy spending time with them. Many caiques like to cuddle or be close to their humans, and they often show their love through gentle nibbling or playful behavior. This makes them a great choice for people who want a bird that is both interactive and loving.

However, their high energy levels mean that caiques need plenty of attention and stimulation. They are intelligent birds that can get bored easily if they don't have enough to do. Providing them with plenty of toys, time outside of their cage, and opportunities to play and interact is important for keeping them happy and healthy.

Overview Of Caiques

Caiques (pronounced "kai-eeks") are a type of parrot that come from South America. There are two main kinds of caiques: the White-Bellied Caique and the Black-Headed Caique. These parrots are medium in size, usually about 9 to 10 inches long. They have strong, stocky bodies and short tails, which give them a sturdy appearance. One of the things that makes caiques stand out is their bright, colorful feathers. Depending on the species, their plumage is a mix of green, orange, yellow, and white, which gives them a unique and eye-catching look.

Caiques are known for their lively and playful personalities. They have a lot of energy and are always on the move, which makes them different from some other types of parrots that may sit quietly for long periods. Caiques love to explore, climb, and play with toys, and they are constantly looking for something fun to do. This high energy level means they are often described as "clowns" of the parrot family. Their behavior can be funny and goofy, making them very entertaining to watch and interact with.

Because they are so active, caiques need plenty of mental stimulation to stay happy and healthy. They are very intelligent birds, which means they can get bored easily if they don't have enough to do. To keep a caique content, it's important to give them a variety of toys and activities to engage with. Owners often provide them with puzzles, climbing structures, and other fun things to keep them entertained. Caiques enjoy figuring out how things work, and they are known to be curious about their surroundings.

In addition to being playful, caiques can also be quite mischievous. Their curiosity sometimes gets them into trouble, as they love to explore and test their environment. They might chew on furniture, get into things they shouldn't, or try to sneak into places they're not supposed to be. For this reason, it's important for owners to supervise them carefully, especially when they are out of their cages.

Despite their mischievous nature, caiques are also very affectionate and form strong bonds with their owners. They enjoy spending time with people and often show their affection through playful behavior, gentle nibbling, or cuddling. Many caiques love being the center of attention and will seek out interaction with their humans. This makes them a good pet for people who want a bird that is both interactive and loving.

However, it's important to note that owning a caique comes with responsibility. Because they are so energetic and intelligent, they require a lot of attention and care. Caiques are not the type of bird that can be left alone in a cage for long periods without becoming bored or unhappy. They need regular time outside of their cage to play and interact with their owners. Without enough stimulation, they can develop behavioral problems like screaming or feather plucking.

In terms of noise, caiques are generally not as loud as some other parrots, but they can still make noise when they are excited or want attention. They are not known for talking as much as other parrot species, but they can mimic sounds and may learn a few words. Their playful nature often makes up for their limited talking ability, as they are still very communicative through their body language and sounds.

History And Origin

Caiques are parrots that come from the tropical forests of South America. You can find them in countries like Brazil, Peru, and Ecuador. In the wild, they live in rainforests and other areas with lots of trees, where they usually form small groups or flocks. The dense, green forests they live in are perfect for caiques because their bright, colorful feathers help them blend into their surroundings, making it easier for them to hide from predators.

Caiques have a varied diet in the wild. They eat different kinds of fruits, seeds, and flowers, depending on what is available in their habitat. Their sharp beaks help them crack open seeds and fruits, and their curious nature leads them to explore different food sources. Living in the lush rainforests, caiques have access to a wide variety of foods, which keeps them healthy and active in their natural environment.

Even though caiques have been part of the natural landscape in South America for centuries, they have only recently become popular pets in other parts of the world. Indigenous people in South America have known about caiques for a long time, but it wasn't until the last few decades that these birds started to be kept as pets in places like North America and Europe. As more people became interested in exotic pets, caiques were introduced to the pet trade, and they quickly became favorites for bird lovers.

One of the reasons caiques have become so popular is their friendly and affectionate nature. Caiques enjoy interacting with humans, and they can form strong bonds with their owners. Many people find their playful and loving personalities to be very appealing, which makes them a great choice for someone looking for a pet that is both fun and affectionate. Unlike some birds that may prefer to be left alone, caiques actively seek attention and enjoy being involved in what's happening around them.

Another reason caiques have gained popularity is their striking appearance. Their feathers are a mix of bright colors, including shades of green, yellow, orange, and white. These vivid colors make caiques stand out from other birds and add to their charm. Many people are drawn to their unique and eye-catching look, which adds to their appeal as pets.

Today, caiques are bred in captivity specifically for the pet market. This means that the birds you see in pet stores or with breeders have been raised in human care, not taken from the wild. Breeding caiques in captivity helps protect wild populations from being harmed or reduced by the pet trade. However, even though they are becoming more common in captivity, caiques are still considered less common than other popular parrot species, like cockatiels or budgies. This rarity makes them even more special to bird enthusiasts who appreciate their unique qualities.

Because they are less common than other types of parrots, caiques are often considered a more "exclusive" pet. Their smaller numbers make them more unique, and many people are excited to have a pet that is not as widely seen as other parrots. Bird lovers who are interested in exotic or rare pets may find caiques to be a perfect choice.

However, owning a caique comes with responsibility. They are active and intelligent birds that need a lot of attention and care. Their curious and playful nature means they require plenty of toys, time out of their cages, and interaction with their owners to stay happy and healthy. Caiques can become bored if they don't have enough mental stimulation, and this can lead to behavioral problems. For someone who is prepared to meet their needs, though, caiques can be incredibly rewarding pets.

Different Types Of Caiques

There are two main types of caiques that people keep as pets: the White-Bellied Caique (Pionites leucogaster) and the Black-Headed Caique (Pionites melanocephalus). Although these two species share many similarities, they do have some differences in how they look and act.

White-Bellied Caiques

As their name suggests, White-Bellied Caiques have mostly white feathers on their bellies. They are very colorful birds, with bright green wings and back. Their legs are orange-yellow, and they also have a touch of orange around their cheeks and head, which gives them a very cheerful and lively look. Their beak is a light, horn color, and they have grey feet.

The White-Bellied Caique's bright and varied colors make them stand out, and many people are drawn to their eye-catching appearance. These birds have a rounded, sturdy body, and their white belly contrasts beautifully with their colorful wings and face. This makes them one of the most visually striking members of the parrot family.

Black-Headed Caiques

Black-Headed Caiques look similar to White-Bellied Caiques in some ways but have one major difference: their head. As the name says, Black-Headed Caiques have an entirely black head, which is the main feature that sets them apart. While they also have bright green wings and orange-yellow underparts like the White-Bellied Caique, their dark head makes them easy to recognize.

Like their White-Bellied cousins, Black-Headed Caiques have a colorful and attractive appearance. The combination of their black head, green wings, and orange-yellow body makes them a striking bird to look at. Many people find their dark heads give them a more distinctive and unique look compared to other parrot species.

Behavior and Personality

Both the White-Bellied and Black-Headed Caiques are known for being very energetic, playful, and curious. These birds are always on the move, exploring their environment, playing with toys, and interacting with their owners. Caiques are often called the "clowns" of the parrot world because they have such fun, silly personalities. They love to hop, climb, and play, and their lively behavior can be very entertaining.

In terms of behavior, there aren't many major differences between the two species. Both types of caiques are highly active and need lots of attention, toys, and activities to keep them happy. They are intelligent birds that enjoy solving puzzles and learning new things, so it's important to keep them mentally stimulated.

That being said, some owners have noticed small differences in personality between the two species. For example, some people say that White-Bellied Caiques tend to be a bit more outgoing and bold. They may be more likely to assert themselves and show a little more confidence when interacting with people and their surroundings. On the other hand, Black-Headed Caiques might be slightly more reserved or cautious in some situations, although they are still very playful and active.

It's important to remember that these differences in personality are often very subtle, and each bird is unique. Even within the same species, individual caiques can have different temperaments based on their experiences, how they are raised, and their personal quirks. Some White-Bellied Caiques might be shy, while some Black-Headed Caiques can be more outgoing—it really depends on the individual bird.

Why Caiques Make Great Pets

Caiques are fantastic pets for people who love birds and want a fun, engaging companion. They have many qualities that make them special and well-loved by their owners. Here are some of the main reasons why caiques are such great pets:

Playful and Energetic

Caiques are full of energy and always ready to play. These birds are very active and love to explore their surroundings. They are curious and like to investigate everything around them. Caiques enjoy playing with toys, climbing, hopping, and interacting with their environment. They are not the kind of parrot that sits still for long periods of time. Caiques love to move around and are happiest when they have plenty of activities to keep them busy.

If you're someone who likes to have a lively and active pet, a caique could be a perfect choice. They enjoy being part of whatever their owners are doing and thrive on action and excitement. Whether they are playing with toys, exploring their cage, or interacting with their owners, caiques are always on the go.

Affectionate Nature

One of the reasons people love caiques so much is their affectionate nature. Caiques form strong bonds with their owners and enjoy spending time with them. They are very social birds that crave attention and interaction. Many caiques love being petted and cuddled by their owners. They often enjoy head scratches and even playful wrestling with their humans.

Caiques are happiest when they have plenty of time to interact with the people they love. They don't like being left alone for long periods of time and can become lonely or bored if they don't get enough attention. If you're looking for a pet that enjoys being close to you and wants to be involved in your daily life, a caique will fit right in.

Entertaining Behavior

Caiques are often called the "clowns" of the parrot world, and for good reason. They have funny, entertaining behavior that makes them a joy to watch. One of the unique things about caiques is how they hop instead of walking. They seem to bounce around with excitement, and it's very fun to watch them move. Caiques also love to dance, and they will often sway back and forth to music or sounds they hear.

Their vocalizations are another source of entertainment. While they don't talk as much as some other parrot species, caiques have their own unique sounds. They make a variety of whistles, squawks, and other noises that are interesting and playful. Some caiques can learn to mimic a few sounds or words, but it's their overall behavior and playful nature that keep their owners entertained.

Intelligent and Trainable

Caiques are highly intelligent birds, and they can be trained to do all kinds of tricks. Because they are so smart, they enjoy learning new things and solving puzzles. Caiques love the mental stimulation that comes from training sessions, and they can be taught to do fun tricks like spinning in a circle, waving, or playing games with their owners.

Their intelligence also means they need regular mental challenges to stay happy. Owners can keep them entertained by providing toys that make them think, such as puzzle toys or games that involve finding hidden treats. Caiques love to explore these challenges and figure things out.

Training a caique can be a very rewarding experience. They are quick learners and enjoy the attention and treats that come with training. Because they are so intelligent, they are eager to please and can form strong connections with their owners during these sessions.

Understanding Caique Temperament

Caiques are known for their bold and confident personalities. Unlike some other birds that may be shy or timid, caiques are very self-assured and assertive. They love to explore their surroundings and will happily express their opinions about things. This strong personality is one of the reasons why caiques are such engaging pets.

However, this confidence can sometimes come off as stubbornness. Caiques are curious birds, and their inquisitive nature can lead them to test boundaries. They may want to explore everything and can get into mischief if not properly supervised. Because of their strong personalities, caiques require patient and consistent training. Owners need to teach them what behaviors are acceptable and what are not. If caiques are not trained well, they may develop bad habits, such as nipping at fingers or becoming territorial over their toys or space.

It's essential to start training early. Caiques are intelligent birds and can learn quickly, but they need guidance to understand the rules of their environment. Positive reinforcement is a great way to train them. This means rewarding good behavior with treats, praise, or attention. By encouraging good behavior and discouraging bad behavior with gentle corrections, caiques can learn what is expected of them.

Another important aspect of caique behavior is their playful and sometimes mischievous nature. Caiques love to play and have fun, which is one of their most endearing qualities. They are always looking for ways to entertain themselves, whether it's playing with toys, climbing on their cage, or interacting with their owners. However, this playful side can also lead to trouble if they are not given enough things to do. If a caique gets bored, they may resort to behaviors that are undesirable, such as excessive noise or chewing on furniture and other household items.

To keep caiques happy and healthy, it's important to provide them with plenty of social interaction and mental stimulation. They are very social creatures and thrive on companionship. Spending time with their owners is essential for their well-being. Regular interaction, whether it's playing games, talking, or just spending time together, helps build a strong bond between the caique and its owner.

Mental stimulation is also vital. Providing toys that encourage problem-solving, such as puzzle toys or foraging toys, can keep caiques engaged and prevent boredom. These toys challenge their minds and help satisfy their natural curiosity. It's a good idea to rotate toys regularly to keep their environment fresh and exciting.

Caiques are also known to be vocal, and they can make a variety of sounds. While they may not talk as much as some other parrots, they do have their unique vocalizations. They might whistle, squawk, or make other noises to express themselves. While some owners find their noise level manageable, it's important to be aware that caiques can be loud at times, especially when they want attention or are excited.

Because they thrive on attention, it's crucial for potential caique owners to be ready to spend time with their birds every day. Caiques do not do well in isolation; they can become lonely or bored if left alone for too long. This loneliness can lead to behavioral problems, which can be challenging for both the bird and its owner.

CHOOSING THE RIGHT CAIQUE

What To Look For In A Healthy Caique

When choosing a caique as a pet, it's very important to make sure the bird is healthy. A healthy caique will live a long, happy, and active life, and adjusting to its new home will be easier if it is in good shape. Here are some key signs to look for when deciding if a caique is in good health:

Bright and Clear Eyes

One of the first things to check when looking at a caique is its eyes. A healthy bird will have bright, clear eyes with no signs of swelling, discharge, or dullness. The eyes should look alert and lively. If the bird's eyes look watery, cloudy, or are showing signs of swelling, this could be a sign that the caique is sick. Healthy eyes are a good indication that the bird is feeling well and isn't suffering from any infections or health problems.

Clean and Vibrant Feathers

A caique's feathers are another important indicator of its health. The feathers of a healthy caique should look smooth, shiny, and well-groomed. The bird should not have any bald patches or areas where the feathers look frayed, broken, or damaged. Additionally, the feathers should be vibrant in color, which reflects the bird's overall well-being.

If a caique's feathers look dull or messy, or if the bird has bald spots, this could be a sign that the bird is stressed, ill, or not getting proper nutrition. Sometimes birds with poor feather condition are also suffering from skin problems, parasites, or other health issues. A well-groomed caique with bright, smooth feathers is likely a healthy bird.

Active and Playful Behavior

Caiques are known for being very active and playful birds. A healthy caique will always be moving around, exploring, playing, and interacting with its environment or people. When you observe a caique, watch for signs of activity. The bird should be climbing around its cage, playing with toys, hopping, and showing curiosity about its surroundings.

If a caique is sitting quietly for long periods, seems uninterested in its surroundings, or appears sluggish or sleepy, it could be sick. While birds sometimes take breaks to rest, a caique that is constantly quiet or inactive might not be feeling well. Healthy caiques have lots of energy and a playful, curious nature.

Good Appetite

Another key sign of a healthy caique is a strong appetite. Caiques love food, and a healthy bird will show enthusiasm when it's time to eat. When choosing a caique, observe how it responds to food. A bird that eagerly eats and seems interested in its food is usually in good health. However, if a caique shows no interest in food, is eating very little, or has lost weight, this could be a sign that something is wrong.

Healthy caiques should be eating a well-balanced diet that includes a variety of fruits, vegetables, and pellets. If the bird appears underweight or shows no interest in eating, it's important to check for underlying health problems.

Clean Vent Area

The vent area (the area under the bird's tail where it eliminates waste) should also be checked for signs of health. A healthy caique will have a clean, dry vent area with no discharge or staining. If the area around the vent looks dirty or there is discharge, this can be a sign of digestive problems, diarrhea, or other health issues.

Keeping an eye on the vent area is important because digestive problems can indicate a number of health concerns, from poor diet to illness. A clean and dry vent area is a good sign that the bird's digestive system is working properly.

Adopting From Breeders Vs. Rescues

When you decide to get a caique, one of the most important choices is whether to adopt from a breeder or a rescue. Both options have advantages and challenges, so it's important to think carefully about which one is the best fit for you.

Adopting from a Breeder

When you adopt a caique from a breeder, you are usually getting a bird that has been raised in a controlled and cared-for environment from a young age. Reputable breeders focus on raising birds that are hand-fed, well-socialized, and used to being around people. This can be a big advantage because the bird is likely to be friendly and comfortable with human interaction right from the start. You are also more likely to adopt a younger bird from a breeder, which means you'll have the chance to bond with your caique from an early age.

Another benefit of working with a breeder is that they can provide you with important information about the bird. A responsible breeder will give you details about the caique's health, diet, and family history. You can also ask the breeder questions about the bird's temperament, which will help you understand what to expect.

However, not all breeders are the same. It's important to make sure you are working with a reputable breeder who treats their birds with care and respect. Avoid breeders who keep their birds in cramped or dirty cages, or who don't seem to care about the well-being of the animals. A good breeder will let you visit their facility, meet the birds' parents, and see the conditions the birds are living in. They will also be happy to answer your questions and provide proper documentation about the bird's health.

Adopting from a Rescue

Adopting a caique from a rescue organization can be a very rewarding experience. Many birds in rescues are there through no fault of their own

— their previous owners may have had life changes that made it impossible to care for them, or the birds might have been neglected. By adopting from a rescue, you are giving a caique a second chance at a happy life in a loving home.

One of the benefits of adopting from a rescue is that many of the birds are already older, which can be a good fit for people who don't want to deal with the high energy and training demands of a young bird. Older caiques might be calmer and may have already learned basic behaviors.

However, adopting from a rescue can come with challenges as well. Birds from rescues may have had difficult past experiences that could affect their behavior. For example, some caiques may be shy, fearful, or have behavioral problems because of past neglect or trauma. These birds may need more time, patience, and understanding to adjust to their new home. It's important to remember that, with love and proper care, many rescued birds can overcome these issues and become wonderful pets.

When adopting from a rescue, it's important to ask about the bird's history and any special needs it might have. A good rescue organization will work closely with you to make sure the bird is a good fit for your home and lifestyle. They will also provide support and guidance to help the bird adjust to its new environment.

Which Option is Right for You?

Whether you choose to adopt from a breeder or a rescue, it's essential to consider your own situation and what you are looking for in a pet. If you want a young caique that has been hand-raised and is comfortable around people from the start, adopting from a breeder might be the best choice. However, make sure you only work with ethical breeders who provide their birds with good care and proper socialization.

On the other hand, if you are open to adopting an older bird or want to give a bird a second chance at a happy life, a rescue might be a great option. While birds from rescues may need more time and patience, the experience of helping a caique overcome its past challenges can be incredibly rewarding.

Male Vs. Female Caiques

When it comes to caiques, there isn't much difference between males and females in terms of personality and behavior. Both male and female caiques are known to be playful, affectionate, and full of energy. Whether you choose a male or female bird, they can both make excellent pets. What matters most is the individual bird's personality, which is shaped more by how they were raised and the environment they live in rather than their gender.

Similar Personalities

Male and female caiques both share the same basic traits that make them such popular pets. Caiques are often described as the "clowns" of the parrot world because they are always active, curious, and entertaining. They love to play with toys, explore their surroundings, and interact with their owners. These lively birds enjoy being the center of attention and can be very affectionate, regardless of whether they are male or female.

Many caique owners agree that their bird's individual personality is what really stands out, not whether they are male or female. Some caiques may be more social and enjoy spending lots of time with their humans, while others might be a bit more independent. This difference in personality is often due to how the bird was raised and the amount of interaction and training it has received rather than its gender.

Minor Differences Between Males and Females

Although male and female caiques are generally very similar, there are some small differences that a few owners have noticed. These differences are usually not very significant and may only show up in certain situations.

For example, some owners report that male caiques can be a little more assertive or territorial at times, especially during breeding season. During this time, male birds may become more protective of their space, toys, or even their owners. They might be more likely to nip or show aggressive behavior if they feel threatened. However, these behaviors are usually temporary and can be managed with proper training and attention.

On the other hand, female caiques are sometimes described as being slightly more reserved than males. This means that they may be a little quieter or less demanding of attention. However, this doesn't mean that female caiques aren't playful or affectionate. In fact, many female caiques are just as lively and loving as their male counterparts. The differences in behavior are often very small, and most caique owners don't notice any significant changes between males and females.

Importance of Personality Over Gender

When choosing a caique, it's important to focus more on the bird's individual personality rather than whether it is male or female. Just like people, each bird has its own unique traits and preferences. Some caiques may be more cuddly and affectionate, while others may be more energetic and independent. These traits can vary greatly between individual birds, regardless of their gender.

The way a bird is raised and trained plays a much larger role in shaping its behavior than whether it is male or female. A caique that has been socialized well and given plenty of attention from a young age is more likely to be friendly and confident around people. On the other hand, a bird that hasn't had much interaction with humans might be more shy or reserved, no matter what its gender is.

Choosing the Right Caique

If you are thinking about getting a caique, it's a good idea to spend time with the bird before making a decision. Whether the bird is male or female, the most important thing is to choose one that matches your personality and lifestyle. Some birds may be more outgoing and playful, while others may be calmer and enjoy quiet time.

Pay attention to how the bird interacts with you and its surroundings. Does it seem curious and friendly, or is it more shy and nervous? These are the things that will determine whether the bird is a good fit for your home, rather than its gender.

Caique Age And Lifespan

Caiques are known for being long-lived birds. On average, they can live between 25 and 30 years in captivity, and with proper care, some caiques may even live longer. Because they have such a long lifespan, owning a caique is a long-term commitment. If you're thinking about getting one, it's important to consider how long the bird will be part of your life. This makes caiques great pets for people who are ready to provide care, attention, and companionship for many years.

Lifespan and Proper Care

The lifespan of a caique depends on the care it receives throughout its life. A healthy diet, regular exercise, mental stimulation, and a safe, clean living environment are all essential to helping your caique live a long and happy life. In the wild, caiques have to rely on their natural instincts to find food and stay safe, but in captivity, they depend on their owners to provide everything they need. With the right care, a caique can thrive and live for many years.

To give your caique the best chance at a long life, it's important to provide a varied diet that includes fresh fruits, vegetables, and high-quality bird pellets. Exercise is also key because caiques are very active birds. Giving them enough space to fly, climb, and play will keep them healthy and prevent obesity and other health problems. Mental stimulation, such as toys and puzzles, is equally important for their well-being, as caiques are highly intelligent and need challenges to stay happy.

Regular visits to a veterinarian who specializes in birds are also essential to monitor your caique's health and catch any issues early. Birds are known to hide signs of illness, so routine check-ups can help ensure that your caique stays in good health.

Choosing a Younger Caique

If you decide to adopt a younger caique, especially one that is under a year old, be prepared for a very energetic and playful bird. Young caiques are full of life and curiosity, and they need a lot of attention and training to learn good behavior. While their high energy levels can be fun, they can also be challenging for owners who are not used to handling such active pets.

Young caiques are at a stage where they are learning about their environment and forming bonds with their owners. This can be a great time to build a strong, trusting relationship with your bird. With consistent training, you can teach your caique important skills, such as how to interact with people, respond to commands, and behave properly around the house.

However, raising a young caique also requires time and patience. These birds need a lot of social interaction and mental stimulation to stay happy. Without enough attention, they may develop bad habits like biting, excessive noise, or destructive behavior. But with the right care and dedication, a young caique can grow into a well-behaved and loving companion.

Choosing an Older Caique

Adopting an older caique can be a good option if you prefer a bird that is a bit more settled. Older caiques have usually passed through their most demanding developmental stages, meaning they may be calmer and more predictable in their behavior. While they still have plenty of energy, they might not require as much attention or training as a younger bird.

One advantage of adopting an older caique is that it may already be trained in basic behaviors. For example, it may be used to interacting with people, playing with toys, and responding to commands. This can make the transition into your home easier, as the bird is already familiar with being around humans and may have fewer behavioral challenges.

Another benefit is that older caiques can still form close relationships with new owners. Even though they may have already bonded with previous caregivers, caiques are social birds that enjoy interacting with people. With time and patience, an older caique can develop a strong bond with you and become a loyal companion.

Preparing Your Home For A Caique

Before bringing a caique into your home, it's important to make sure your space is set up to meet their needs. Caiques are very active, curious birds, and they need a safe, fun environment where they can explore, play, and interact. Here are some key things to consider when preparing your home for a caique:

Cage Size and Setup

One of the most important things your caique will need is a spacious cage. Caiques are medium-sized parrots, and they need plenty of room to move around, climb, and play. The minimum cage size for a caique is 24x24x30 inches, but bigger is always better. A larger cage will give your bird more space to stay active and engaged. Make sure the cage has horizontal bars, as caiques love to climb.

Inside the cage, it's important to have several perches placed at different heights so your caique can rest and move around easily. You'll also want to include toys, swings, ladders, and other items that allow your bird to explore and stay entertained. Caiques are very intelligent and need variety in their environment to prevent boredom.

Toys and Mental Stimulation

Caiques are known for being playful and full of energy, so having plenty of toys in their cage is a must. They enjoy chewing, climbing, and solving puzzles, so provide a variety of toys to meet these needs. Chew toys, such as wood blocks or natural ropes, are great for helping them keep their beaks healthy while giving them something to focus on.

Foraging toys, where the bird has to work to get a treat or find hidden food, are also a good way to keep your caique's mind busy. Puzzle toys, where they have to solve something to get a reward, are another excellent option. Since caiques are intelligent birds, rotating their toys regularly helps keep them interested and engaged. This means swapping out old toys with new ones every few days to give them something fresh and exciting to play with.

Safety Considerations

Caiques are very curious and love to explore their surroundings, so it's important to make sure your home is bird-proofed to keep them safe. This means taking steps to remove any potential hazards. For example, you'll want to keep electrical cords out of reach or covered, as caiques might try to chew on them, which can be dangerous.

Small objects, like jewelry, rubber bands, or buttons, should be kept away, as birds may swallow them by accident. Make sure that any toxic plants or household chemicals, like cleaning products, are stored in a place where your bird can't get to them. You should also check that windows and doors are secure so your caique doesn't accidentally escape when flying around the house.

If you plan to let your caique out of the cage for some free-flight time, make sure the room is safe for them to explore. Remove anything that could hurt them, like sharp objects or small spaces where they could get stuck. Close windows and doors to prevent accidents.

Time and Attention

Caiques are very social birds, and they need a lot of attention from their human companions to stay happy and healthy. If they don't get enough interaction, they can become bored or stressed, which may lead to behavioral problems like excessive screaming, biting, or destroying things in their environment.

To prevent this, be prepared to spend time with your caique every day. They enjoy playing games, learning tricks, or just being in the same room with you. Training sessions can also be a fun way to bond with your bird and provide mental stimulation. Caiques can learn to do tricks, like waving or turning around, and they often enjoy the challenge of learning something new.

Even when you're busy, try to make sure your caique can see you and feel like they are part of the family. Simply having them out of their cage, sitting nearby, or allowing them to watch what you're doing can help them feel included.

Chapter 2

SETTING UP THE PERFECT HABITAT

Cage Size And Bar Spacing Requirements

When preparing a home for a caique, one of the most important things to consider is choosing the right cage. Caiques are very active, playful birds that need a lot of space to move around, climb, and exercise. To keep your caique happy and healthy, you'll need to select a cage that meets their size and safety needs.

Cage Size

Caiques are small to medium-sized parrots, but despite their size, they are full of energy. They need a cage that is big enough to give them room to explore, stretch their wings, and play. The minimum recommended cage size for a caique is 24x24x30 inches. This provides enough space for them to move around, but if you have the room, it's always better to go for a larger cage. A bigger cage will give your caique even more space to stay active and avoid boredom.

If you plan on keeping more than one caique in the same cage, a larger size is especially important. Multiple birds need extra space to avoid feeling cramped, as this can lead to stress and behavior problems. Birds in too-small cages may become aggressive or start picking at their feathers. A larger cage allows each bird to have its own area to play and rest.

Bar Spacing

In addition to cage size, the spacing between the bars of the cage is very important for your caique's safety. Caiques are curious and love to climb, and they will often explore every part of their cage. For this reason, the bars need to be spaced correctly to prevent any accidents. If the bars are too wide, the bird might get its head or body stuck, which can cause injury or even death.

The ideal bar spacing for caiques is between 5/8 inch and 3/4 inch. This range ensures that the bars are close enough together to keep your bird safe but still wide enough for the bird to climb and grip comfortably. Anything wider than this could pose a risk, while bars that are too narrow might make the cage feel cramped.

Why Size and Bar Spacing Matter

A cage that is too small or has unsafe bar spacing can cause both physical and mental harm to your caique. If a cage is too small, the bird won't be able to get enough exercise, which can lead to obesity, muscle loss, and other health problems. It can also lead to boredom, which may cause behavioral issues such as screaming, biting, or feather plucking.

Caiques are known for their playful, active nature, and they need enough space to express this energy. A large cage gives them room to jump, flap their wings, and play with toys, helping them stay physically fit and mentally stimulated. Plus, a spacious cage can reduce stress and make the bird feel more at ease in its environment.

Bar spacing is equally important. Birds can easily get hurt if the bars are too wide, as their heads or bodies might get stuck while trying to climb. This can lead to panic, injury, or worse. Proper bar spacing prevents these accidents, ensuring that your caique can explore the cage safely.

Adding Perches, Toys, and Accessories

Once you have the right cage size and bar spacing, it's important to fill the cage with items that will make your caique feel at home. Perches of different sizes and textures are essential for keeping your bird's feet healthy and giving them places to rest. Toys are also important for mental stimulation. Caiques love to play with chew toys, puzzle toys, and things they can climb on.

Make sure the cage setup allows your caique to move around freely. Avoid overcrowding the cage with too many accessories, which can take up valuable space for your bird to move and exercise. The goal is to provide enough enrichment to keep your caique busy without making the cage feel cramped.

Cage Location And Environment

After choosing the right cage for your caique, it's just as important to pick the best spot in your home to place it. Caiques are social birds that love being around people and part of the action, so where you put their cage can affect their happiness and well-being. However, it's essential to balance this with making sure they aren't in a stressful or unsafe environment.

Here's how to create the ideal space for your caique:

A Social but Calm Area

Caiques are curious and social creatures. They enjoy watching people and being involved in daily activities. Therefore, it's best to place their cage in a room where family members spend a lot of time, such as the living room or family room. This way, your caique will be able to see and hear what's going on, feel included, and stay entertained.

However, while caiques like being social, they also need a calm environment. Avoid placing the cage in a spot that is too busy, noisy, or chaotic. For instance, putting the cage near the TV or a sound system could cause stress from loud sounds. Additionally, sudden movements or loud noises may frighten your bird, which can affect their health and mood. A quiet corner of the living room where there's moderate activity is usually a good balance.

Avoid the Kitchen and Harmful Fumes

Never put your caique's cage in the kitchen. The kitchen can be a dangerous place for birds due to cooking fumes, especially from non-stick cookware, which can release harmful chemicals. Also, kitchens often have a lot of sudden noise, heat, and activity, all of which can stress out your bird.

Stay Away from Direct Sunlight and Drafts

Birds love some sunlight, but direct exposure for long periods can lead to overheating. Make sure that the cage is not in a spot where the sun shines directly on it for several hours a day, like right next to a window. Too much heat can make your bird uncomfortable or sick. Instead, pick a place with indirect sunlight, so they can enjoy some natural light without being in the sun's full glare.

Also, avoid placing the cage near windows, doors, or air vents where there might be drafts or sudden temperature changes. Birds are sensitive to cold air, and being in a drafty spot could make your caique sick. Temperature changes can also affect their comfort, so it's best to keep the cage in a location with stable conditions.

Stable Temperature

Caiques are happiest in temperatures between 65°F and 80°F. If the temperature in the room goes too high or too low, your bird could become stressed or ill. Keep the cage in a room where the temperature stays within this range. Avoid placing the cage near heaters, air conditioners, or fireplaces, as these can create uncomfortable temperature fluctuations.

Finding the Right Height

Another important factor to consider is the height of the cage. Birds naturally feel safer when their cage is elevated, so it's a good idea to place the cage on a stand or table. A height where the bird's perch is at your chest or eye level is ideal. This allows the bird to feel more secure and be more comfortable interacting with people.

However, don't place the cage too high, as it could make it difficult for you to interact with or check on your caique. It's also important to keep the cage away from other pets, like cats or dogs, who might frighten or try to reach the bird. Make sure the cage is in a place where your caique can enjoy a safe view of their surroundings without feeling threatened.

Final Tips

To ensure your caique is happy and comfortable in its new home, it's important to regularly observe the environment and adjust if needed. Pay attention to how your bird responds to its cage placement. If it seems stressed, constantly hiding, or not eating well, it might be a sign that the cage is in the wrong spot.

Additionally, provide a quiet spot in the cage where your bird can retreat if it needs rest or privacy. Caiques enjoy a busy household, but they also need downtime. Offering a cozy corner with a perch or hideaway will give your bird a sense of security and a place to relax.

Perches And Cage Furnishings

When setting up a cage for your caique, perches and other furnishings are key to keeping your bird healthy, comfortable, and happy. Caiques need places to rest, exercise, and play. Perches are essential because they give the bird a spot to stand and help keep their feet in good condition. If you include a variety of perches, it can mimic the natural environment they would have in the wild. This variety helps prevent foot problems, such as sores or arthritis.

Here's a guide on how to choose the right perches and cage furnishings for your caique:

Types of Perches to Include

1. Natural Wooden Perches

Natural wooden perches are one of the best choices for your caique. These perches are made from natural tree branches, which give your bird different textures to grip. This is good for their feet because it strengthens the muscles and helps wear down their nails naturally. The uneven surface also helps prevent foot sores by making sure the bird doesn't put too much pressure on one part of its foot.

In addition to being great for their feet, wooden perches allow caiques to chew on them. Chewing is a natural behavior for birds, and it helps keep their beak healthy. However, you need to be careful about the type of wood you use. Some woods are toxic to birds, like cedar and pine. Safe choices include eucalyptus, apple, manzanita, and willow branches. Always check that the wood is untreated and free from pesticides or harmful chemicals before placing it in your bird's cage.

2. Rope Perches

Rope perches are another excellent option for your caique. These perches are soft and comfortable, making them a great place for your bird to rest its feet. Caiques love to climb, and rope perches can give them a new surface to explore. The soft texture is also gentle on their feet, providing a change from the harder surfaces of wooden perches.

However, it's important to make sure the rope is tightly woven. Loose or frayed threads can be dangerous, as your bird could get tangled or accidentally ingest them. Regularly check the condition of the rope perches, and replace them if you notice signs of wear or fraying.

3. Perches of Different Sizes

In the wild, birds land on branches of all different shapes and sizes, so it's important to replicate that in their cage. Providing perches of varying diameters will help exercise your caique's feet. A mixture of thick and thin perches gives them the chance to use different muscles, which keeps their feet healthy and prevents foot problems.

Large, thicker perches provide a stable place for resting, while smaller, thinner perches encourage the bird to grip tightly, helping strengthen their feet. By giving them different perch sizes, you add variety to their environment and prevent boredom, keeping your bird engaged and active.

Additional Cage Furnishings

Beyond perches, your caique's cage needs other items to make it a safe and comfortable home. Here are a few things to include:

1. Food and Water Bowls

Your bird will need bowls for food and water. The best choice is stainless steel bowls because they are durable, easy to clean, and resistant to bacteria. Caiques can be messy eaters, so it's important to clean their food and water bowls daily to prevent germs from growing. Avoid using plastic bowls, as they can scratch easily, creating spots where bacteria can grow.

2. Toys and Enrichment

Caiques are intelligent and energetic birds, so they need plenty of toys to keep them busy and prevent boredom. Include toys for chewing, such as wood blocks or shreddable paper. Foraging toys, where the bird has to solve a puzzle to get a treat, are also great for mental stimulation. Make sure to rotate the toys regularly to keep your bird interested.

3. Ladders and Swings

In addition to perches, consider adding ladders and swings to your caique's cage. Ladders provide extra climbing opportunities, which caiques love, while swings give them something fun to play on and enjoy the motion. These items also add variety to the environment, encouraging your bird to stay active and explore.

4. Cage Lining

Finally, make sure to line the bottom of the cage with bird-safe paper or another easy-to-clean material. This will catch droppings and make daily cleanup simpler. Avoid using materials like sandpaper or corncob bedding, as they can be harmful if ingested.

Toys And Enrichment Items

Caiques are very smart birds, and they need a lot of mental stimulation to stay happy and healthy. Without enough toys and activities, caiques can become bored, which might lead to bad behaviors like feather plucking, excessive screaming, or chewing on things they shouldn't. To keep your caique entertained and engaged, it's important to provide a variety of toys and enrichment items. Below are some types of toys that will help keep your caique active and happy.

1. Foraging Toys

Foraging toys are designed to encourage your caique to use its problem-solving skills. These toys usually have hidden treats or food inside that your bird needs to find. By figuring out how to access the treats, your caique engages its mind and body, which is essential for mental stimulation. These toys can keep your bird busy for hours, helping to reduce boredom and anxiety. You can buy foraging toys from pet stores or make your own by hiding treats in cardboard boxes or paper bags. Just be sure that whatever you use is safe for your bird to chew on.

2. Chew Toys

Caiques love to chew, and providing plenty of chew toys is important for their well-being. Chewing is a natural behavior that helps keep their beaks healthy and trim. You can find many types of chew toys, such as wooden blocks, soft wood, and shreddable toys made from safe materials. Look for toys made from bird-safe woods like apple, pine, or balsa. Always check the toys for signs of wear and replace them regularly to ensure they are safe for your bird. Having a variety of chew toys will keep your caique satisfied and happy.

3. Climbing Toys

Caiques are active birds that enjoy climbing. To keep your caique physically active, include climbing toys like ladders, swings, and ropes in their cage. These toys provide your bird with opportunities to climb, exercise, and explore. A swing can be a fun place for your caique to play, while ladders give them more places to move around in their cage. Ropes are also great because they can climb and perch on them comfortably. Make sure these toys are securely attached to the cage to prevent any accidents.

4. Interactive Toys

Interactive toys are excellent for keeping your caique engaged. These toys can move or make sounds, which makes them exciting for your bird to play with. Examples include bells, balls, and hanging toys that swing or spin. Caiques enjoy batting at things, so toys that roll or bounce can be very entertaining. These toys encourage your bird to be active and playful, allowing them to express their natural instincts.

5. Rotating Toys

To keep your caique interested in their toys, consider rotating them regularly. By changing the toys every week or so, you can keep your bird curious and excited. This rotation prevents them from getting bored with the same toys, providing a fresh environment for exploration and play. When you remove some toys, be sure to put them back later so your caique can rediscover them.

6. Safety Considerations

When choosing toys for your caique, it's crucial to ensure they are made from bird-safe materials. Avoid toys with small parts that could be swallowed, or those made with toxic materials like certain plastics or paints. Always check the labels and look for toys specifically designed for birds.

Cleaning And Maintenance Of The Habitat

Keeping your caique's cage clean is very important for its health and happiness. A clean cage helps prevent the buildup of bacteria, mold, and bad smells, which can make your bird sick. Regular cleaning and maintenance also create a nice living environment for both you and your caique. Here are some simple tips for cleaning and maintaining your bird's habitat effectively.

Daily Cleaning

Every day, you should do some basic cleaning to keep your caique's cage fresh. Start by removing any uneaten food from the food bowls. This helps prevent spoilage and keeps the cage tidy. Next, clean the water bowls. It's important for your caique to have fresh, clean water every day, so make sure to wash the bowls with warm, soapy water and rinse them well before refilling them.

After that, spot-clean any messes on the cage floor or perches. Caiques can be quite playful and may leave droppings or food scraps behind. Use paper towels or a soft cloth to wipe up any messes you see. This daily cleaning helps keep the cage looking good and reduces odors.

Weekly Cleaning

In addition to daily cleaning, you should do a more thorough cleaning once a week. Start by removing all the toys, perches, and other accessories from the cage. This gives you full access to the cage and makes it easier to clean.

Use warm water and a bird-safe disinfectant to clean the cage bars, the floor, and any accessories. It's important to avoid using harsh chemicals like bleach, as these can be toxic to your bird. A good disinfectant designed for bird cages will help eliminate bacteria and odors without harming your caique.

After you've cleaned everything, dry the cage thoroughly before putting the toys and perches back in. This helps prevent moisture buildup, which can lead to mold growth.

Replace Bedding or Tray Liners

If you use bedding or paper to line the bottom of the cage, it's important to replace it regularly. This prevents odors and keeps the cage clean. Depending on how messy your caique is, you might need to change the bedding every week or even more frequently. Choose bird-safe bedding materials, like paper or aspen shavings, and avoid any that could be harmful to your caique.

Perch and Toy Inspection

While cleaning, take the time to inspect the perches and toys. Look for any signs of wear or damage. Over time, toys can break or become frayed, and perches can get worn down. If you see any worn or broken toys, it's important to replace them right away to keep your caique safe.

Check the perches for any sharp edges or splinters that could harm your bird's feet. Make sure all toys are intact and free from any small parts that could be swallowed. Regular inspections help ensure that your caique has a safe and fun environment to play in.

General Tips for a Clean Habitat

1. Location Matters: Place the cage in an area that is easy to access for cleaning. A central location in your home allows you to keep an eye on your caique while you clean and interact with it regularly.

2. Keep Cleaning Supplies Handy: Have all your cleaning supplies in one place, including bird-safe disinfectant, paper towels, and a soft cloth. This way, you'll be prepared to clean whenever you need to.

3. Set a Cleaning Schedule: Establish a regular cleaning schedule to help you remember when to clean daily and weekly. You can set reminders on your phone or keep a chart to track your cleaning tasks.

4. Make It a Routine: Include your caique in the cleaning process when it's safe to do so. Some birds enjoy being part of the activity, and it can be a bonding experience for you both.

NUTRITION AND DIET

Basic Dietary Needs Of Caiques

Caiques are omnivores, meaning they eat a variety of foods that come from both plants and animals. To keep your caique healthy and happy, it's important to provide a balanced diet that includes several key types of foods. Here's a simple guide to the dietary needs of caiques:

1. Fruits and Vegetables

Fruits and vegetables should make up a large part of your caique's diet. These foods are packed with essential vitamins, minerals, and antioxidants that help keep your bird healthy. Here are some good choices for fruits and vegetables:

• Fruits: Apples (without seeds), bananas, berries (like strawberries and blueberries), grapes, mangoes, and melons are all excellent options. Make sure to wash fruits thoroughly and remove any seeds or pits before feeding.

• Vegetables: Offer a variety of vegetables such as carrots, bell peppers, broccoli, leafy greens (like kale and spinach), and peas. These are all nutritious and will provide important nutrients for your caique.

When feeding fruits and vegetables, aim for fresh produce whenever possible. You can serve them chopped or in larger pieces for your caique to explore and enjoy. Remember to introduce new foods gradually, as some caiques may be hesitant to try unfamiliar items.

2. Seeds and Nuts

Seeds and nuts are another important part of a caique's diet, but they should be given in moderation. While they are high in fat and provide energy, too many can lead to obesity and other health issues.

Good choices for seeds include sunflower seeds, pumpkin seeds, and millet. Nuts like almonds and walnuts can also be offered as treats. Make sure they are unsalted and unseasoned. Because seeds and nuts are high in fat, it's best to limit these to a small amount, such as a few nuts or a small handful of seeds a few times a week.

3. Pelleted Diets

High-quality pelleted diets are essential for caiques. Pellets are specially formulated to provide all the nutrients your caique needs to stay healthy. They are balanced and contain the right mix of vitamins, minerals, and proteins.

When selecting pellets, look for those specifically designed for caiques or small to medium-sized parrots. Pellets should make up a significant portion of your caique's daily diet, as they offer a consistent source of nutrition. Always ensure your caique has access to fresh pellets every day, and check the packaging for the recommended serving size based on your bird's weight and activity level.

4. Protein Sources

Protein is also an important part of your caique's diet. Caiques benefit from various protein sources that support muscle development and overall health. Here are some good protein options:

• Cooked Beans and Legumes: Black beans, kidney beans, and lentils are excellent choices. Make sure to cook them thoroughly and avoid adding any salt or seasoning.

• Eggs: Occasionally offering small amounts of cooked eggs (scrambled or hard-boiled) can provide a protein boost.

• Cooked Meat: While not a major part of their diet, small pieces of cooked chicken or turkey can be given as an occasional treat.

Fresh Fruits And Vegetables

Fresh fruits and vegetables are very important for a caique's diet. They provide essential vitamins, minerals, and hydration that keep your bird healthy and active. Below are some recommended fruits and vegetables, along with tips on how to safely prepare them for your caique.

Fruits

Caiques love to eat a variety of fruits. Here are some good options you can offer:

1. Apples: Caiques enjoy apples, but make sure to remove the seeds, as they can be harmful. Wash the apple thoroughly to get rid of any pesticides or chemicals before feeding it to your bird.

2. Pears: Pears are also a favorite among caiques. Just like apples, remember to wash them well and remove any seeds before giving them to your bird.

3. Berries: Blueberries, strawberries, and raspberries are nutritious and delicious options. They are small and easy for caiques to eat. Rinse them well before serving.

4. Bananas: Caiques often enjoy the sweet taste of bananas. You can slice them into small pieces to make them easier for your bird to eat.

5. Grapes: Grapes can be a fun treat for caiques. They are juicy and hydrating.

Wash them thoroughly, and you can either serve them whole or cut them in half to make them easier to eat.

6. Mangoes: Caiques usually love mangoes. Make sure to remove the pit and cut the fruit into small, manageable pieces. Rinse the mango before serving.

7. Papayas: This tropical fruit is also a great option for caiques. Peel the papaya and remove the seeds, then cut it into bite-sized pieces.

When offering fruits to your caique, always wash them thoroughly to remove any harmful pesticides or chemicals. It's best to remove any seeds, pits, or skins that could be dangerous for your bird. Introducing new fruits gradually is important. This way, you can monitor your caique's reaction and ensure it doesn't have any digestive issues.

Vegetables

Vegetables are another important part of a caique's diet. Here are some excellent choices:

1. Leafy Greens: Kale, spinach, and collard greens are packed with nutrients and should be included in your caique's diet. Wash them well and chop them into small pieces to make it easier for your bird to eat.

2. Carrots: Carrots are crunchy and sweet, making them a tasty treat for caiques. You can serve them raw by cutting them into thin slices or grating them. Cooked carrots are also an option, but make sure they are cooled down before offering.

3. Sweet Potatoes: These are rich in vitamins and can be served cooked and mashed or cut into small, soft pieces. Make sure they are plain without any seasoning.

4. Broccoli: Broccoli is a nutritious vegetable that caiques often enjoy. You can serve it raw or lightly steamed. Cut it into small florets for easy eating.

5. Bell Peppers: Caiques love the sweet taste of bell peppers. You can offer them in various colors—red, yellow, or green. Wash and cut them into small strips or pieces.

6. Zucchini: This soft vegetable is another great choice for caiques. You can serve it raw or cooked, sliced into small, bite-sized pieces.

When offering vegetables, it's best to chop them into small, manageable pieces. This makes it easier for your caique to eat and reduces the risk of choking. Always introduce new vegetables gradually, just like with fruits, to observe how your bird reacts.

Freshness is Key

It's crucial to always provide fresh fruits and vegetables to your caique. Avoid giving them wilted or spoiled produce, as this can lead to health problems. Regularly check the fruits and vegetables you offer and replace any that have gone bad.

Seeds, Nuts, And Pellets: What's Best?

When it comes to feeding your caique, understanding the roles of seeds, nuts, and pellets in their diet is essential. While seeds and nuts can be tasty treats, they should not be the main part of your caique's diet. Here's a breakdown of how to properly incorporate these foods into your caique's meals.

Seeds and Nuts

Seeds and nuts can be delicious for caiques, but they are high in fat. If caiques eat too many fatty foods, they can become overweight, which can lead to health problems. Therefore, seeds and nuts should only be given as occasional treats rather than as a daily food.

1. Seeds: A varied seed mix can be offered to your caique a few times a week. Look for a mix that includes seeds like sunflower seeds, pumpkin seeds, and millet. Always remember that seeds should not make up the bulk of your caique's diet.

2. Nuts: Unsalted nuts, such as almonds, walnuts, and pistachios, can be a great reward for your bird. Nuts are nutritious, but because they are high in fat, only offer a small amount. A few nuts a week is enough to satisfy your caique without risking obesity.

Using seeds and nuts as rewards for good behavior or during training sessions can be an effective way to bond with your caique. Just be sure to keep portion sizes small to avoid overfeeding.

Pelleted Diets

Pelleted diets are highly recommended for caiques. These pellets are specially formulated to provide a complete and balanced diet, ensuring your bird gets all the nutrients it needs.

1. Choosing the Right Pellets: Look for high-quality pellets that are made for caiques or other small to medium-sized parrots. The best pellets will contain a mix of grains, fruits, and vegetables. Avoid brands that include artificial colors, preservatives, or additives, as these can be harmful to your bird.

2. How Much to Feed: Pellets should make up about 60-70% of your caique's daily food intake. This ensures they receive the vitamins and minerals necessary for good health.

Transitioning to Pellets

If your caique is used to a diet of mostly seeds, it may take time for them to accept pellets. Here's how to help your bird make the transition:

1. Gradual Introduction: Start by mixing a small amount of pellets with their current diet of seeds. For example, if you usually give them one cup of seed mix, add a tablespoon of pellets to it.

2. Increase Pellets Slowly: Over the course of a week or two, gradually increase the number of pellets while decreasing the seeds. Monitor how your caique reacts. Some birds will accept pellets quickly, while others may take longer to adjust.

3. Be Patient: If your caique refuses to eat pellets at first, don't worry. It's common for birds to prefer seeds over pellets. Keep offering them alongside their usual food, and eventually, your caique may start trying the new pellets.

4. Make it Fun: You can try offering pellets in different ways, such as hiding them in foraging toys or mixing them with favorite fruits or veggies. This can encourage your bird to taste the pellets.

Foods To Avoid

When feeding your caique, it is important to know which foods are safe and which ones can be harmful. Some foods can be toxic to caiques and can cause serious health issues. Here is a list of foods that should always be avoided:

1. Avocado

Avocado is a popular fruit among people, but it is very dangerous for birds.

It contains a substance called persin, which is toxic to caiques and other birds. Even a small amount of avocado can cause serious health problems, including heart issues and respiratory distress. It's best to keep all avocado products out of your caique's reach.

2. Chocolate and Caffeine

Chocolate and caffeinated drinks like coffee and tea are also highly toxic to caiques. These substances can lead to severe health problems, including heart problems and even death. Even small amounts of chocolate can be dangerous, so it's essential to keep all chocolate and caffeinated products away from your bird.

3. Alcohol

No amount of alcohol is safe for caiques. Alcohol can cause serious health problems in birds, including liver damage and death. It is crucial to ensure that your caique does not have access to any alcoholic beverages or food items that may contain alcohol.

4. Onions and Garlic

Onions and garlic, whether raw, cooked, or powdered, should never be given to caiques. These foods can damage a bird's red blood cells, leading to anemia and other serious health issues. It's important to avoid any food items that contain onions or garlic, including some sauces, soups, and prepared foods.

5. High-Fat and Salty Foods

Foods that are high in fat, salt, or sugar can be harmful to caiques. This includes snacks like chips, processed foods, and fast food. These foods can lead to obesity, heart disease, and other health problems in your bird. Instead, focus on providing a healthy diet that includes fresh fruits, vegetables, and high-quality pellets.

6. Certain Fruits

While many fruits are safe and healthy for caiques, some can be harmful due to their pits or seeds. For example, fruits like cherries and peaches contain pits that can be dangerous if ingested. Always remove any seeds or pits from fruits before offering them to your caique. It's also a good idea to wash fruits thoroughly to remove any pesticides or chemicals.

7. Other Harmful Foods

In addition to the items mentioned above, there are other foods that should be avoided. Some of these include:

• Rhubarb: The leaves of the rhubarb plant are toxic to birds.

• Certain Beans: Raw kidney beans can be toxic to birds. Always cook beans before offering them to your caique.

• Mushrooms: Some mushrooms are toxic and can cause serious health issues. It's best to avoid feeding mushrooms to your caique altogether.

• Dairy Products: Birds are generally lactose intolerant, so it's best to avoid giving them dairy products like milk or cheese.

Keeping Your Caique Safe

To keep your caique safe and healthy, it is important to know which foods are harmful and to avoid feeding them any of the items listed above. Always check the ingredients in any food you offer your bird, and when in doubt, it's best to stick to foods that are known to be safe.

Establishing A Feeding Routine

Setting up a regular feeding routine for your caique is important for their health and happiness. Birds thrive on consistency, and having a schedule can help reduce stress and encourage good eating habits. Here are some tips to help you establish an effective feeding routine for your caique:

1. Daily Feeding Schedule

It's best to offer fresh food to your caique at the same times every day. Most caiques do well with two main feedings: one in the morning and one in the evening. This schedule mimics their natural feeding habits in the wild, where they tend to forage for food in the morning and late afternoon. Sticking to a daily feeding routine can also help your bird know when to expect meals, making them feel more secure.

2. Provide Fresh Water

Clean, fresh water should always be available for your caique. Make sure to change the water daily to keep it clean and free of bacteria. You can use a water bottle or a bowl, but whichever you choose, ensure it is easy for your bird to access. Regularly checking the water supply is essential, as caiques can be very active and may drink more water when they're playing and exploring.

3. Monitor Food Intake

Keeping track of how much food your caique eats each day is crucial. Monitoring their food intake can help you adjust portion sizes based on their eating habits and activity level. If your caique is not eating well or if you notice a change in their eating patterns, it's important to consult an avian veterinarian. They can help determine if there are any health issues affecting your bird's appetite.

4. Introduce Variety

Caiques enjoy variety in their diet, so it's a good idea to introduce new foods regularly. Rotate different fruits and vegetables throughout the week to keep their meals interesting. This not only provides a range of nutrients but also stimulates your caique's curiosity and encourages them to try new things. You can also switch up the types of pellets or seeds you offer from time to time to prevent boredom and ensure they get a balanced diet.

5. Treats in Moderation

While seeds and nuts can be tasty treats for your caique, they should not be the main part of their diet. High-fat foods can lead to obesity and other health issues if given too often. Instead, use seeds and nuts as occasional rewards or treats. This approach will help maintain your caique's health and keep them from becoming overweight.

6. Observe Your Caique's Preferences

Every caique has its own preferences when it comes to food. Some might love certain fruits, while others may prefer specific vegetables. Pay attention to what your caique enjoys the most, and try to include those foods in their diet. This will make mealtime more enjoyable for them and can encourage better eating habits.

7. Clean Feeding Dishes Regularly

Keeping your caique's feeding dishes clean is just as important as providing fresh food and water. Dirty dishes can harbor bacteria and lead to health problems. Clean the food and water dishes daily, and wash them with warm, soapy water. Rinse thoroughly to remove any soap residue, and allow them to dry before refilling them.

8. Be Patient and Adaptable

Establishing a feeding routine may take time, especially if your caique is new to your home. Be patient and give your bird time to adjust to the new schedule. Some caiques may be picky eaters at first, but with persistence and encouragement, they will likely adapt to the routine. Be flexible and willing to adjust the routine if necessary, especially if you notice changes in your bird's behavior or preferences.

3

Chapter 3

HEALTH AND WELLNESS

Common Health Issues In Caiques

Caiques, like all pets, can experience a range of health issues during their lives. Understanding these common health problems is important, as it allows you to take steps to prevent them and seek prompt treatment when needed. Here are some typical health issues that caiques may face:

1. Obesity

Caiques love to eat, and if their diet is not managed carefully, they can easily become overweight. Obesity is a serious concern for caiques because it can lead to various health problems. These include heart disease, liver issues, and joint problems. To prevent obesity, it is crucial to provide a balanced diet, limit treats, and ensure your caique has plenty of opportunities to exercise. Regular playtime and mental stimulation are important to keep them active and healthy.

2. Feather Plucking

Feather plucking, also known as feather-destructive behavior, is when a caique pulls out its own feathers. This behavior can be caused by several factors, including stress, boredom, or underlying health issues. Feather plucking can lead to severe feather loss and skin infections, which can be painful for your bird. If you notice your caique plucking its feathers, it is important to investigate the cause. Providing mental enrichment, social interaction, and a stable environment can help reduce stress and prevent this behavior.

3. Respiratory Infections

Caiques are sensitive to poor air quality and can develop respiratory infections if they are exposed to irritants. Common signs of respiratory infections include sneezing, coughing, wheezing, and labored breathing. If you notice any of these symptoms, it is essential to take your caique to a veterinarian as soon as possible. To help prevent respiratory infections, maintain a clean living environment, avoid smoking near your bird, and ensure that your home is well-ventilated.

4. Gastrointestinal Problems

Caiques can experience digestive issues, such as diarrhea or vomiting, due to changes in their diet, infections, or parasites. These symptoms can be serious and require immediate attention from a veterinarian. It's essential to monitor your caique's droppings and overall health regularly. If you notice any changes in their stool consistency or if your bird is vomiting, contact a veterinarian right away. To help prevent gastrointestinal problems, provide a balanced diet, introduce new foods gradually, and ensure your bird stays hydrated.

5. Skin and Beak Problems

Caiques can develop skin infections, beak deformities, or overgrowth if their environment is not properly maintained or if they do not have appropriate materials to chew on. Skin problems can arise from poor hygiene or lack of proper nutrition. To keep your caique's skin and beak healthy, provide safe chewing materials, such as natural wood perches and toys, and maintain a clean living environment. Regularly check your caique's beak and skin for any signs of issues, such as redness, swelling, or unusual growths, and consult a veterinarian if you notice anything concerning.

6. Prevention and Regular Check-ups

Preventing health issues in caiques involves regular veterinary check-ups, a balanced diet, and a clean living environment. Routine vet visits can help catch any health problems early before they become serious. Your veterinarian can also provide vaccinations and treatments for common health issues.

Ensuring your caique has plenty of toys, perches, and activities will help keep them mentally and physically stimulated, reducing the likelihood of behavioral issues like feather plucking.

Signs Of Illness And When To Call A Vet

Caiques are known for being lively and playful birds, but they can be good at hiding their discomfort and illness. As a responsible pet owner, it is important to keep a close eye on your caique's behavior and appearance. Noticing any changes can help you identify potential health issues early. Here are some common signs of illness in caiques that you should watch for:

1. Changes in Appetite

One of the first signs that something might be wrong with your caique is a change in its appetite. If your bird suddenly stops eating or drinking, or if you notice a significant decrease in the amount of food it consumes, this could indicate a health problem. Caiques are naturally curious and enjoy exploring different foods, so a sudden disinterest in food can be a red flag. If your caique refuses to eat for more than a day, it is important to contact your veterinarian.

2. Lethargy

Lethargy is another important sign to watch for. If your caique is less active than usual, spends more time sitting quietly, or seems to lack interest in play and interaction, it may not be feeling well. Caiques are generally energetic and playful, so a noticeable drop in energy or engagement can be concerning. If your bird seems unusually tired or reluctant to move around, it's best to consult a vet.

3. Changes in Vocalization

Caiques are known for their vocal nature, and any changes in their vocalization can be significant. An increase in vocalization, such as more loud squawking, can indicate distress or discomfort. Conversely, a decrease in vocalization may suggest that your caique is feeling unwell. Pay close attention to your bird's usual sounds and patterns; if you notice any significant changes, it could be a sign of a problem.

4. Physical Changes

Physical changes in your caique can also signal health issues. Look for signs such as:

• Weight Loss: If your bird appears to be losing weight, it's important to investigate. You can monitor your caique's weight by weighing it regularly.

• Fluffed Feathers: Birds often fluff their feathers when they are cold or unwell. If your caique's feathers are puffed up for an extended period, it may be feeling sick.

• Dirty or Matted Vent Area: A clean vent area is a sign of good health. If you notice that this area is dirty or matted, it could indicate digestive issues or other health problems.

• Discharge: Any discharge from your caique's eyes or nostrils should be taken seriously. It could indicate a respiratory infection or another health issue.

5. Behavioral Changes

Changes in behavior can also be significant. If your caique becomes more aggressive, withdrawn, or exhibits unusual behaviors, it may be a sign of stress or illness. For instance, if a normally friendly bird becomes aggressive or bites more often, it may be in pain or feeling unwell. Similarly, if your caique starts to hide or avoid interaction, this behavior change could indicate a health issue that needs attention.

6. When to Call the Vet

If you notice any of the signs mentioned above, it is important to take action. Always err on the side of caution when it comes to your caique's health. If your bird shows any signs of illness, it is best to consult a veterinarian who specializes in avian care. Some issues can escalate quickly, so timely intervention can make a big difference in your bird's health.

Parasites And Disease Prevention

Caiques, like other birds, can get sick from parasites and diseases. To keep your caique healthy, it is important to take steps to prevent these issues. Here are some effective ways to minimize the risks of parasites and diseases for your caique:

1. Regular Veterinary Check-ups

One of the best ways to keep your caique healthy is by scheduling annual check-ups with a veterinarian who specializes in birds, known as an avian vet. During these check-ups, the vet will perform thorough examinations and screenings to check for any parasites or diseases. Regular check-ups are essential because they help detect health problems early, making it easier to treat any issues that arise. This proactive approach can save your bird from serious health complications in the future.

2. Maintain a Clean Environment

Keeping your caique's cage and living area clean is very important for preventing diseases. A dirty cage can lead to the buildup of bacteria, mold, and parasites, which can make your bird sick. Here are some cleaning tips to follow:

• Daily Cleaning: Remove any uneaten food and clean the water bowls every day. Spot clean any messes on the cage floor and perches to maintain hygiene.

• Weekly Deep Cleaning: Once a week, take out all toys, perches, and accessories from the cage. Use warm water and a bird-safe disinfectant to clean the cage bars, floor, and accessories. Avoid using harsh chemicals like bleach, as they can be toxic to birds.

• Replace Bedding and Tray Liners: If you use bedding or paper to line the bottom of the cage, replace it regularly. This helps prevent odor and keeps the living environment clean.

By maintaining a clean environment, you reduce the risk of bacterial infections and parasites that can affect your caique's health.

3. Quarantine New Birds

If you decide to bring a new bird into your home, it is crucial to quarantine it for at least 30 days. Quarantining means keeping the new bird separate from your existing caique during this time. This practice allows you to monitor the new bird's health and ensure it does not carry any diseases or parasites that could be harmful to your caique. After the quarantine period, you can gradually introduce the new bird to your caique, keeping a close eye on both birds' health during the transition.

4. Avoid Wild Birds

Wild birds can carry diseases and parasites that may be harmful to your caique. It is best to avoid letting your bird interact with or be in areas where wild birds frequent. If you have an outdoor aviary, make sure it is properly secured to prevent wild birds from entering. Additionally, keep windows and doors closed when wild birds are nearby to avoid accidental encounters.

5. Proper Diet and Nutrition

A balanced and nutritious diet is essential for your caique's overall health and immune system. Ensure that your caique has access to fresh fruits, vegetables, high-quality pellets, and occasional seeds or nuts. A strong immune system can help your bird fight off potential illnesses and infections. Always provide fresh water and monitor your caique's eating habits to ensure it is maintaining a healthy diet.

6. Monitor Behavior and Health

Pay close attention to your caique's behavior and health. Look out for any signs of illness, such as changes in appetite, lethargy, or unusual vocalizations. If you notice any concerning symptoms, consult your veterinarian immediately. Quick action can prevent minor issues from becoming serious health problems.

Grooming And Bathing Your Caique

Grooming and bathing are essential parts of keeping your caique healthy and happy. Regular grooming helps maintain your bird's feathers and can prevent problems like feather plucking. Here are some important grooming tips to help you take care of your caique:

1. Beak and Nail Care

Checking your caique's beak and nails regularly is important for its overall health. Here's how to manage their care:

- Nail Trimming: If your caique's nails get too long, they might need to be trimmed. Long nails can cause discomfort and may lead to injuries. If you're not sure how to trim nails safely, it's best to consult a veterinarian or an experienced bird groomer. They can show you the proper technique and help you avoid cutting too close, which can cause bleeding. If you do decide to trim your bird's nails yourself, use special bird nail clippers and be careful to only cut the tip of the nail.
- Beak Care: Regularly check your caique's beak for any signs of overgrowth or damage. A healthy beak should be smooth and not too long. If you notice that the beak is excessively long or misshapen, take your bird to the vet for evaluation.

2. Feather Care

Caiques generally do not require regular feather trimming, but it's still important to monitor their feathers. Here are some tips:

- Inspect for Damage: Regularly check your caique's feathers for any damage or broken feathers. Damaged feathers can lead to discomfort and may cause your bird to pluck them out. If you notice any broken feathers, it may be best to consult a professional avian groomer or vet to have them removed safely.
- Feather Condition: Ensure your caique's feathers are clean and free from dirt. A clean feather coat helps insulate and protect your bird from temperature changes.

3. Bathing

Bathing is an important part of grooming and helps keep your caique's feathers clean and healthy. Most caiques enjoy bathing, and there are different ways to provide bath time:

- Shallow Dish: You can offer a shallow dish of water for your caique to bathe in. Make sure the water is shallow enough that your bird can splash around without risk of drowning. Some caiques love to soak in the water, while others prefer to dip their toes and splash around.
- Misting: Alternatively, you can use a fine mist spray bottle to give your caique a gentle shower. Hold the bottle a few feet away and lightly mist your bird. This can mimic rain, which many birds naturally enjoy. Be careful not to

spray directly in your caique's eyes or face, as this can be uncomfortable for them.

• Bathing Frequency: Bathing can be done a few times a week, depending on your bird's preference. Some caiques may enjoy bathing every day, while others may only want to bathe once a week. Pay attention to your bird's behavior to see how often it prefers to bathe.

4. Supervision During Bathing

Always supervise your caique during bath time. While most birds enjoy bathing, it's important to ensure they are safe. Make sure the bathing area is secure and free from any hazards.

• Drying Off: After your caique is done bathing, it will likely shake off excess water, which is perfectly normal. If it is cold or drafty in your home, consider placing your caique in a warm area or using a soft towel to gently dry it off. Avoid using a hairdryer, as the noise can be stressful for your bird.

5. Additional Grooming Considerations

• Positive Reinforcement: Make grooming a positive experience for your caique. Use treats and praise to encourage your bird to enjoy the grooming process. This will help your caique associate grooming with positive experiences.

• Regular Grooming Sessions: Try to establish a regular grooming routine. Frequent handling and gentle grooming can help your caique become more comfortable with the process. This is also a great way to bond with your bird.

First Aid For Your Parrot

Knowing basic first aid for your caique can be extremely helpful in emergencies. Being prepared can make a big difference in keeping your bird safe and healthy. Here are some common situations you may encounter with your caique and how to respond effectively:

1. Minor Cuts and Scrapes

If your caique gets a minor cut or scrape, follow these steps:

• Clean the Wound: Gently clean the area around the wound with a mild saline solution or warm water. This helps remove dirt and bacteria that could cause infection.

· Antiseptic Application: If you have a bird-safe antiseptic, apply a small amount to the wound. Avoid using human antiseptics, as they may contain harmful ingredients.

· Monitor for Infection: Keep an eye on the injury over the next few days. Watch for signs of infection, such as increased redness, swelling, or discharge. If the wound does not heal properly or seems to worsen, consult an avian veterinarian for advice.

2. Bleeding

If your caique has a bleeding injury, it's important to act quickly:

· Apply Pressure: Use a clean cloth to apply gentle pressure to the bleeding area. This helps slow or stop the bleeding.

· Calm Your Bird: Keep your caique calm and quiet during this time. Stress can increase heart rate and blood flow, making it harder to stop the bleeding.

· Seek Veterinary Help: If the bleeding does not stop within a few minutes, seek veterinary assistance immediately. Persistent bleeding can be dangerous and may require professional care.

3. Choking

If you suspect that your caique is choking, look for signs like gasping, flapping, or visible distress:

· Hold the Bird Carefully: Gently hold your caique, ensuring you have a secure but comfortable grip.

· Tilt Forward: Tilt the bird slightly forward to help dislodge the object.

· Gentle Taps: Give a few gentle taps on its back with your other hand. This can help encourage the object to come loose.

· Veterinary Care: If your bird does not recover quickly or if it continues to show signs of distress, seek veterinary care immediately. Choking can be life-threatening if not addressed quickly.

4. Poisoning

If you suspect that your caique has eaten something toxic, such as avocado or chocolate, take the following steps:

· Immediate Action: Contact an avian veterinarian right away. Time is critical in cases of poisoning.

• Details to Provide: Be prepared to give details about what your bird ate, how much, and when it happened. This information can help the vet determine the best course of action.

5. Heat Stroke

Heat stroke can occur if your caique is exposed to high temperatures, especially in warm weather:

• Signs of Heat Stress: Look for symptoms like panting, lethargy, or fluffed feathers. These indicate that your bird may be overheating.

• Move to a Cooler Area: Immediately take your caique to a cooler environment, away from direct sunlight. This can help lower its body temperature.

• Offer Water: Provide fresh, cool water to help keep your bird hydrated. Encourage it to drink, but do not force it.

• Veterinary Advice: If the symptoms persist or if your caique seems unwell after being cooled down, contact a veterinarian for further advice.

BONDING WITH YOUR CAIQUE

Building Trust And Rapport

Building trust with your caique is essential for creating a strong bond between you and your bird. It takes time and patience, but the rewards are well worth the effort. Here are some effective strategies to help you establish a good relationship with your caique:

1. Create a Safe Environment

The first step in building trust is to ensure that your caique feels safe in its surroundings. Here's how you can do that:

• Comfortable Cage: Make sure the cage is spacious and comfortable. Include appropriate perches and toys that allow your bird to climb, explore, and play. The more comfortable and engaged your caique is, the more relaxed it will feel.

• Quiet Living Area: Keep the living area calm and quiet. Avoid placing the cage in noisy or busy areas of your home. Sudden loud noises can frighten your caique and make it feel insecure. A peaceful environment helps your bird feel safe and more open to interaction.

2. Respect Their Space

When first getting to know your caique, it's important to give it some space:

• Observe from a Distance: Allow your caique to observe you from a distance. At first, let it watch you without forcing any interaction. This will give your bird time to become familiar with your presence.

• No Forceful Interaction: Avoid grabbing or holding your caique when it doesn't want to be handled. Instead, wait for your bird to come to you on its own. This helps your caique learn that it can trust you to respect its boundaries.

• Encourage Exploration: Once your caique feels more comfortable, encourage it to explore its surroundings. You can sit near the cage and talk softly to it, allowing it to come closer at its own pace.

3. Use Positive Reinforcement

Positive reinforcement is a powerful tool for building trust:

• Treats and Praise: Use treats and praise to reward your caique for any interaction with you. When your bird comes closer, offer a favorite snack or use a gentle voice to praise it. This helps your caique associate you with good experiences.

• Gradual Approach: Start with small rewards for small steps, such as just moving closer to you or allowing you to touch it gently. As your bird becomes more comfortable, you can gradually increase the level of interaction.

• Consistency Matters: Be consistent with your rewards. Each time your caique shows curiosity or takes a step toward you, acknowledge its effort with a treat or kind words. This encourages your bird to keep trying and builds trust over time.

4. Establish a Consistent Routine

Birds thrive on routine, and having a consistent schedule can help your caique feel more secure:

• Regular Feeding Schedule: Feed your caique at the same times every day. A predictable feeding schedule makes your bird feel safe and reduces anxiety.

• Cleaning and Interaction: Along with feeding, maintain a consistent routine for cleaning the cage and interacting with your bird. Whether it's morning or evening, having a regular time for play or talking can strengthen your bond.

• Daily Interactions: Spend a few minutes each day engaging with your caique, whether through talking, gentle touch, or playtime. This consistent interaction fosters a sense of trust and comfort.

Understanding Caique Body Language

Caiques are expressive birds that communicate a lot through their body language. Understanding these signals is essential for building a strong bond with your caique and knowing how they feel. Here are some common behaviors to look for and what they mean:

1. Feather Position

The position of your caique's feathers can tell you a lot about how it feels:

• Fluffed Up Feathers: If your caique's feathers are fluffed up, this usually means it is relaxed and comfortable. A bird in this state may be resting or enjoying its surroundings.

• Tight Feathers: If you notice your caique's feathers are tight against its body, this can indicate that it is feeling scared, stressed, or uncomfortable. When a bird feels threatened, it tries to make itself appear smaller, which can include pulling its feathers close.

2. Head Bobbing

Head bobbing is a common behavior in caiques that shows excitement or happiness:

• Excited Bobbing: When your caique bobs its head up and down, it is often expressing joy or eagerness to interact. This can happen when you enter the room or when it sees you approaching. It's a positive sign that your caique is ready to play or engage.

• Interaction: You can encourage this behavior by responding positively. Try talking to your caique or offering it a treat when it bobs its head. This strengthens your connection and makes your bird feel more comfortable with you.

3. Tail Position

The position of your caique's tail can also provide insight into its emotions:

• Raised Tail: A caique that has its tail raised is likely feeling playful and curious. This position shows that your bird is excited and ready to explore its environment or interact with you.

• Lowered Tail: Conversely, a lowered tail can indicate fear or submission. If your caique's tail is drooping, it may feel insecure or anxious. It's important to observe the surrounding environment to see if there is something causing this reaction.

4. Nipping and Biting

Caiques are naturally playful and may nip or bite during interactions:

• Gentle Nipping: A light nip can be a playful gesture. Caiques often explore their surroundings with their beaks, and this can include nipping at your fingers or clothes. If your bird nips you gently, it may just be trying to engage in play.

• Excessive Biting: However, if your caique bites hard or frequently, it may be a sign of fear, discomfort, or irritation. Pay attention to the context—if your bird bites when you try to pick it up or if it seems distressed, it's important to give it some space. Understanding the difference between playful nips and distress signals is crucial for your caique's well-being.

5. Vocalizations

Caiques are vocal birds that use different sounds to express their feelings:

• Cheerful Chattering: Happy caiques often chatter and make cheerful sounds. This can include whistling or soft chirps. If your caique is vocal and seems active, it's likely in a good mood.

• Loud Screeching: Loud screeching or whining can indicate discomfort, boredom, or a need for attention. If you hear these sounds, check on your caique to see if it needs something, like more interaction or a change in its environment.

The Importance Of Social Interaction

Caiques are social birds that need interaction with their owners and other birds to stay happy and healthy. Regular social interaction is vital for their emotional well-being. Here are some key reasons why social interaction is important for caiques:

1. Emotional Well-Being

Caiques thrive on companionship. When they get enough social interaction, they become more confident and less likely to develop behavioral issues. Birds that are isolated or lonely may engage in unwanted behaviors, such as:

• Feather Plucking: This is when a bird pulls out its feathers due to stress, boredom, or anxiety.

• Excessive Screeching: If a caique feels neglected or bored, it might scream to get attention.

Engaging with your caique regularly helps meet its social needs and keeps it emotionally balanced. A happy and confident caique is less likely to experience these issues.

2. Cognitive Stimulation

Caiques are intelligent birds that require mental stimulation to stay engaged. Interactive play and socializing with you provide the necessary mental challenges they need. Here are a few ways to stimulate your caique's mind:

• Toys and Puzzles: Offer toys that encourage problem-solving, like foraging toys, which require your bird to work for treats.

• Games: Play simple games with your caique, such as hide and seek or fetch with safe toys.

When caiques do not get enough stimulation, they can become bored and restless. Boredom can lead to destructive behaviors, such as chewing on furniture or other inappropriate items, or they may become withdrawn and less active. Keeping your caique mentally engaged will help prevent these negative behaviors.

3. Strengthening Your Bond

Spending time with your caique builds a strong bond between you and your bird. The more quality time you share, the deeper your connection will grow.

Here are some activities that can help strengthen your bond:

• Talking: Spend time talking to your caique. Birds love to hear their owners' voices. This helps your caique feel secure and loved.

• Playtime: Engage in play with your bird using toys or games. This not only provides physical exercise but also makes your caique feel happy and cherished.

• Cuddling and Petting: Many caiques enjoy gentle petting and snuggling. This physical contact reinforces trust and affection.

A strong bond will lead to a more content and trusting caique. It will feel secure in your presence and may be more willing to engage in social interaction.

4. Positive Reinforcement

Regular interaction with your caique helps create positive associations. When your bird receives attention and affection from you, it learns to associate you with fun, safety, and companionship. Here's how you can encourage positive reinforcement:

• Treats: Use healthy treats to reward your caique for interacting with you. This will create a positive connection between your presence and good experiences.

• Praise: Always offer praise when your caique engages with you. A happy tone of voice and enthusiastic words will encourage your bird to seek out your company.

How To Handle A Shy Or Fearful Caique

When you bring a new caique into your home, it may be shy or fearful, especially in the beginning. It's essential to be gentle and patient with your bird to help it feel comfortable. Here are some tips to help you handle a shy or fearful caique:

1. Go Slow

If your caique seems scared, the best approach is to take things slowly. Moving too quickly can frighten your bird and make it more anxious. Allow your caique time to adjust to its new environment. Here's how you can do this:

- Give Space: Let your bird settle in without forcing interaction. Stay nearby but avoid reaching into the cage right away.
- Observe: Watch your bird's behavior. Let it explore its cage and surroundings at its own pace.

This gradual approach helps your caique feel secure, allowing it to gain confidence in its new home.

2. Use Gentle Movements

When interacting with a shy caique, it's important to be calm and gentle. Sudden movements can startle your bird, making it more fearful. Here are some ways to ensure your movements are soothing:

- Slow and Steady: Move slowly and avoid quick gestures. This will help your caique feel more at ease.
- Soft Voice: Speak softly to your bird. A gentle tone will reassure it that you are not a threat.
- Avoid Loud Noises: Keep the environment calm. Try to minimize loud sounds, such as music or shouting, that might scare your bird.

Being calm helps create a peaceful atmosphere, allowing your caique to feel safe and more willing to interact.

3. Create a Safe Space

It's crucial to provide a safe space for your caique where it can retreat if it feels overwhelmed. This safe area helps your bird feel secure. Here's how to create a comfortable environment:

- Quiet Corner: Designate a quiet spot in its cage or room where your caique can feel safe. This could be a covered area or a cozy nook.
- Hideouts: You can add small shelters, like a bird tent or a hut, where your caique can go when it needs a break.
- Familiar Items: Include familiar toys or perches to make the area feel like home.

Having a safe space will help your caique feel more confident and less anxious in its surroundings.

4. Encourage Exploration

To help your shy caique feel more comfortable, you can encourage it to explore its environment. Here are some ways to do this:

• Use Toys: Place interesting toys around the cage to stimulate curiosity. Chewing and playing can help your bird gain confidence.

• Treats: Offer your bird its favorite treats to entice it to come closer. Place a treat on your hand or nearby to encourage it to approach.

• Positive Reinforcement: When your caique shows interest in exploring or approaches you, offer praise or rewards. This will reinforce its behavior.

Encouraging exploration helps your caique learn that its environment is safe and enjoyable.

5. Be Patient

Building trust with a shy or fearful caique takes time, so it's important to be patient. Here are some tips for fostering a trusting relationship:

• Celebrate Small Victories: Acknowledge even the smallest steps your bird takes, like coming closer to you or accepting a treat from your hand.

• Consistent Interaction: Spend time with your caique daily, even if it's just sitting nearby. Consistent presence helps your bird become familiar with you.

• Avoid Forcing Interactions: Never try to force your caique out of its cage or into interaction. Allow it to approach you when it feels ready.

Bonding Activities For Parrot And Owner

Bonding with your caique is essential for building a strong and loving relationship. Engaging in fun activities together can help deepen your connection. Here are some enjoyable bonding activities you can try with your caique:

1. Training Sessions

Training your caique can be a rewarding way to bond. Teaching your bird simple commands or tricks provides mental stimulation and strengthens your relationship. Here's how to make training sessions effective:

• Start with Simple Commands: Begin with basic commands like "step up" or "spin." These are easy for caiques to learn and can be fun to practice.

• Use Positive Reinforcement: Reward your caique with treats and praise when it follows your command. This encourages good behavior and makes learning enjoyable.

- Keep Sessions Short: Aim for short training sessions of about 5 to 10 minutes. Caiques have short attention spans, so frequent, brief sessions are more effective.

Training not only helps your caique learn new skills but also creates a sense of teamwork between you and your bird.

2. Interactive Play

Playtime is a great way to bond with your caique. Engaging your bird in interactive play can keep it physically active and mentally stimulated. Here are some fun ideas for play:

- Toys: Use various toys such as balls, ropes, or foraging toys to encourage your caique to explore and play. You can toss the ball gently to your bird or dangle a rope for it to climb.
- Encourage Exploration: Let your caique investigate new toys at its own pace. You can join in the fun by moving toys around or making them swing.
- Play Together: Interact with your bird by using toys alongside it. This not only keeps your bird engaged but also strengthens your bond as you share fun experiences.

Playtime can be a great way to build trust and create joyful moments together.

3. Out-of-Cage Time

Allowing your caique to spend time outside its cage is crucial for its well-being and helps with bonding. Here's how to make out-of-cage time enjoyable:

- Supervised Exploration: Find a safe, bird-proofed area for your caique to explore. Make sure there are no hazards like open windows, sharp objects, or dangerous plants.
- Interactive Environment: Place toys and perches in the area to encourage exploration. You can also sit nearby and encourage your caique to come to you for treats or play.
- Enjoy Nature: If possible, take your caique outside (in a secure cage or harness) to enjoy fresh air and sunlight. This new environment can be exciting and help strengthen your bond.

Out-of-cage time allows your caique to explore and interact with you in a new setting, which can be enriching for both of you.

4. Shared Bathing

Many caiques love to bathe, making it a fun activity to do together. Bathing can be an enjoyable bonding experience for you and your bird. Here are some tips for shared bathing:

• Misting: Use a fine mist spray bottle to lightly mist your caique with water. Many birds enjoy this refreshing experience and may even play in the mist.

• Shallow Dish: Provide a shallow dish or bowl filled with water for your caique to splash around in. Make sure the water is shallow enough for safety.

• Supervise Bath Time: Always watch your bird during bath time to ensure it is safe and comfortable. Join in the fun by gently splashing water or encouraging your bird to play.

Bathing together can be a delightful way to bond and keep your caique's feathers clean and healthy.

5. Quality Time

Spending quality time with your caique is essential for reinforcing your bond. Here are some ways to enjoy time together:

• Talk and Sing: Simply sitting with your caique and talking or singing to it can help strengthen your connection. Caiques often enjoy the sound of your voice.

• Relaxed Environment: Create a calm atmosphere where you can be together. You can read, watch TV, or play music while your caique is with you.

• Gentle Touch: If your caique is comfortable, you can offer gentle pets or scratches. Many birds enjoy this form of affection and it can enhance your bond.

4

Chapter 4

BASIC TRAINING TECHNIQUES

Positive Reinforcement Training

Positive reinforcement training is a great way to teach your caique new behaviors and commands. This method focuses on rewarding your bird for doing what you want, which makes it more likely to repeat those behaviors. Here's how to effectively implement positive reinforcement training with your caique:

1. Choose High-Value Rewards

The first step in positive reinforcement training is to find treats that your caique really loves. These treats should be special and exciting to your bird. Here are some suggestions:

• Fresh Fruit: Small pieces of fruit like apple, banana, or grapes can be very motivating for caiques.

• Nuts: Unsalted nuts like almonds or walnuts can also be great rewards. Just remember to give them in moderation because they are high in fat.

• Specialized Bird Treats: Look for bird treats specifically made for caiques or small parrots. These often contain ingredients that birds enjoy.

The key is to select rewards that make your caique excited and eager to participate in training.

2. Timing is Key

When training your caique, timing is crucial. You want to give the reward immediately after your bird does the desired behavior. This helps your caique make a connection between the action and the reward. Here's how to do it:

• Immediate Reward: As soon as your caique performs the behavior you want, such as stepping up onto your hand or ringing a bell, give it the treat right away.

• Positive Association: This immediate response reinforces the behavior, letting your caique know that it did something good.

3. Be Consistent

Consistency is vital in training. Use the same cues and commands every time you train. Here's why consistency matters:

• Clear Understanding: If you always use the same word or phrase for a command, your caique will learn to associate that word with the action.

• Reduced Confusion: Changing commands or rewards can confuse your bird and slow down its learning process.

For example, if you want to teach your caique to "step up," always use that exact phrase. Avoid using different phrases like "come here" or "get up" for the same action.

4. Keep Sessions Short

Caiques have short attention spans, so it's essential to keep training sessions brief. Here's how to structure your sessions:

• Limit to 5-10 Minutes: Aim for training sessions that last around 5 to 10 minutes. This keeps your caique engaged and prevents boredom.

• Frequent Sessions: Instead of one long session, try to have several short sessions throughout the day. This repetition helps reinforce learning without overwhelming your bird.

5. End on a Positive Note

Ending training sessions on a good note is important for your caique's motivation and confidence. Here are some tips:

• Finish with Success: Conclude each training session with a success, even if it's a simple task that your caique can easily accomplish. This could be as simple as having it step up onto your hand or doing a simple trick it already knows.

- Encouragement: Celebrate this success with lots of praise and a tasty treat. This helps your caique feel good about the session and eager for the next one.

Teaching Step-Up And Step-Down Commands

Teaching your caique the step-up and step-down commands is important for handling your bird safely and effectively. These commands allow you to move your caique between different surfaces, like its cage, your hand, or a perch. Here's a simple guide on how to teach these commands.

Step-Up Command

The step-up command is the first command you should teach your caique. Here's how to do it:

1. Get Your Bird's Attention

To start, make sure your caique is calm and focused on you. Here's how to position yourself:

- Hand Position: Hold your hand at your bird's level with your palm facing up. This makes it easier for your caique to see your hand and understand what you want.

2. Introduce the Command

Once you have your bird's attention, it's time to introduce the command:

- Say the Command: In a clear and friendly voice, say "step up." Your tone should be encouraging to help your caique feel comfortable.
- Use Your Finger or Perch: You can also use your finger or a perch to encourage your bird to step onto your hand.

3. Encourage Movement

If your caique doesn't step up right away, you can gently encourage it:

- Gentle Pressure: Lightly press your finger against your caique's belly. This gentle touch can help prompt your bird to step up onto your hand.
- Be Patient: It might take a few tries, especially if your caique is new to this command. Don't rush; give your bird time to understand what you want.

4. Reward

When your caique finally steps onto your hand, it's essential to reward it right away:

• Offer a Treat: As soon as your caique steps up, give it a treat. This can be a small piece of fruit, a nut, or any favorite bird treat.

• Praise Your Bird: Along with the treat, use a cheerful voice to praise your caique. This helps reinforce the behavior and makes your bird associate stepping up with positive experiences.

5. Repeat

Practice the step-up command regularly:

• Consistency is Key: The more you practice, the more your caique will learn to respond reliably to the command.

• Short Sessions: Keep the training sessions short, around 5-10 minutes, so your caique stays engaged and doesn't get bored.

Step-Down Command

After your caique learns to step up, it's time to teach the step-down command. Here's how to do that:

1. Use the Same Approach

You can use a similar method to teach the step-down command:

• Hold Your Hand or Perch: Position your hand or a perch in front of your caique, as you did when teaching the step-up command.

2. Introduce the Command

Now it's time to introduce the step-down command:

• Say the Command: As you encourage your bird to step off your hand, say "step down" in a clear voice.

3. Encourage the Behavior

If your caique hesitates to step down:

• Gentle Guidance: You can gently guide your bird off your hand with your finger. This helps your caique understand what you want it to do.

4. Reward

When your caique successfully steps down, it's important to reward it:

• Praise and Treat: Immediately offer praise and a treat when your bird steps down. This positive reinforcement will help your caique associate the step-down command with a reward.

5. Practice

Just like with the step-up command, practice the step-down command regularly:

· Repetition: Repeat the process until your caique understands both commands well.

Training Your Caique To Come When Called

Training your caique to come when called is an important skill. It can help strengthen your bond with your bird and ensure its safety. Here's a simple guide on how to teach your caique this valuable command.

1. Choose a Cue Word

The first step in training your caique is to select a cue word or phrase that you will use consistently:

· Simple Command: Choose a short and easy phrase like "come here" or just "come." Make sure it is something you will remember and use every time.

2. Start in a Quiet Environment

Begin your training sessions in a calm, distraction-free area:

· Quiet Space: Choose a room where there are no loud noises or other pets that might distract your caique. A quiet environment helps your bird focus on you and the training.

3. Get Your Bird's Attention

To help your caique understand that you want it to come to you:

· Use a Treat: Hold a treat in front of your bird to draw its attention. This could be a small piece of fruit or a favorite seed. The treat should be something your caique really likes.

4. Call Your Bird

Once you have your bird's attention, it's time to give the command:

· Use Your Cue Word: Clearly say your chosen cue word, like "come here." Use a friendly and encouraging tone to make your caique feel comfortable.

· Extend Your Hand: As you say the command, extend your hand with the treat. This gesture shows your bird where you want it to go.

5. Reward and Praise

When your caique approaches you, it's important to reward it immediately:

• Give the Treat: As soon as your bird comes to you, give it the treat. This reinforces the idea that coming when called results in a reward.

• Offer Enthusiastic Praise: Use a happy and encouraging voice to praise your caique. Saying things like "good job!" or "well done!" will make your bird feel appreciated and motivated to respond again.

6. Practice Gradually

As your caique learns to come when called, you can gradually increase the challenge:

• Different Distances: Start calling your caique from a short distance, then slowly increase the distance as it becomes more comfortable.

• New Environments: Once your caique understands the command in a quiet room, try practicing in different areas of your home. You can even take your training outside, as long as it's safe. This helps your bird learn to respond in various situations.

7. Be Patient

Training your caique takes time and patience:

• Every Bird is Different: Some caiques may learn quickly, while others may take longer. It's important to be patient and not rush the process. If your bird doesn't come right away, don't get frustrated.

• Consistent Practice: Regular practice is key to success. Try to have short training sessions each day, ideally 5-10 minutes long. This keeps your caique engaged and helps reinforce what it learns.

Training: What It Is Target And How To Use It

Target training is a fun and effective way to teach your caique to follow and touch a specific object, such as a stick or your finger. This technique can help with different behaviors, including moving to different places and stepping up. Here's a simple guide on how to implement target training with your caique.

1. Choose a Target

The first step in target training is to select a target that your caique can easily see and recognize:

• Target Selection: You can use a small, brightly colored stick, a spoon, or even your finger as the target. Make sure it is something that stands out and is easy for your bird to spot.

2. Introduce the Target

Once you have your target, it's time to introduce it to your caique:

• Hold the Target: Place the target in front of your caique at its eye level. This will make it easier for your bird to see and approach the target.

• Encourage Investigation: Allow your caique to investigate the target. Use a cue word like "target" in a friendly tone to help your bird understand what you want it to do.

3. Reward for Contact

When your caique interacts with the target, it's important to reward it right away:

• Touching the Target: As soon as your caique touches the target with its beak, immediately provide a treat and offer praise. This positive reinforcement encourages your bird to repeat the behavior.

• Praise: Use a cheerful voice to say things like "Good job!" or "Well done!" This will make your caique associate the action of touching the target with positive experiences.

4. Practice Regularly

To ensure your caique understands the target training, consistent practice is essential:

• Repetition: Repeat the process several times during each training session. Aim for short sessions of about 5-10 minutes, as caiques have short attention spans.

• Gradually Increase Distance: Once your caique reliably touches the target, start moving the target a little further away. This will help your bird learn to come to the target from different distances.

5. Incorporate into Commands

Once your caique gets the hang of target training, you can use it to help with other commands, such as step-up and step-down:

• Using the Target with Commands: For example, if you want your caique to step onto your hand, hold the target in front of your hand. When your bird moves to touch the target, it will naturally step up onto your hand.

• Guiding Your Bird: You can also use the target to guide your caique to its perch. Just hold the target near the perch and encourage your bird to follow it.

Handling Nipping And Biting Behavior

Nipping and biting are common behaviors in caiques, especially during training or when being handled. Understanding why your caique nips or bites is important in managing these behaviors effectively. Here are some strategies to help you handle nipping and biting in a positive way.

1. Recognize Triggers

To manage nipping, it's essential to know what causes it:

• Identify the Situation: Observe when your caique tends to nip. Does it happen during handling, when your bird feels scared, or while playing? By understanding the situation, you can respond better and avoid triggering these behaviors in the future.

• Keep a Journal: Sometimes, it can be helpful to keep a record of when nipping occurs and what was happening at that time. This can help you spot patterns.

2. Stay Calm

How you react to nipping can influence your caique's behavior:

• Avoid Sudden Reactions: If your caique nips you, try to stay calm. Do not react with sudden movements or loud sounds, as this can startle your bird and may reinforce the behavior.

• Speak Softly: Use a gentle tone when you speak to your caique after a nip. This can help soothe your bird and reduce stress.

3. Redirect Behavior

If your caique is nipping while playing or during handling, you can redirect its attention:

• Use Toys: Offer your caique a toy to play with instead of your hand. If your bird starts nipping at your fingers, quickly provide a toy for it to focus on.

• Treats as Distractions: Offering a treat can also help shift your caique's focus away from nipping. This way, your bird learns that engaging with toys or treats is more rewarding than biting.

4. Use Positive Reinforcement

Positive reinforcement is a great way to encourage gentle behavior:

• Reward Gentle Interactions: When your caique interacts with you softly, immediately give it treats and praise. This reinforces good behavior and teaches your bird the difference between gentle play and nipping.

• Celebrate Small Successes: If your caique resists the urge to nip in a situation where it usually would, give it lots of praise and rewards. This helps build a positive association with gentle behavior.

5. Give Space

Sometimes, your caique may need space to feel comfortable:

• Recognize Signs of Discomfort: If your caique seems agitated or uncomfortable, it's important to give it some space. Signs of discomfort can include puffed feathers, fast movements, or a tense posture.

• Avoid Forcing Interaction: If your caique is showing signs of stress, don't force it to interact with you. Allow your bird to calm down on its own. Forcing contact can lead to more nipping or biting.

6. Seek Professional Help

If nipping and biting become a frequent problem, it might be time to seek help:

• Consult a Behaviorist: An avian behaviorist can offer valuable insights and strategies tailored to your caique's specific behavior.

• Talk to a Veterinarian: If you notice that the biting is aggressive or seems to be getting worse, consult your vet. They can check for any underlying health issues that might be causing the behavior.

ADVANCED TRAINING AND TRICKS

Teaching Your Caique To Talk

Caiques are known for their ability to make sounds and mimic words. While not every caique will become a chatterbox, you can encourage your bird to talk with patience and practice. Here are some simple steps to help you teach your caique to talk.

1. Start with Simple Words

The first step in teaching your caique to talk is choosing the right words:

• Choose Easy Words: Begin with short and simple words or phrases. Good examples include "hello," "bye-bye," or your caique's name. These words are easy for your bird to learn and use.

• Use Words Frequently: Make sure to use these words often in your daily conversations with your caique. The more your bird hears these words, the more likely it is to learn them.

2. Use Repetition

Repetition is key when teaching your caique to talk:

• Repeat Regularly: Say the chosen words repeatedly during your interactions. Consistent repetition will help your caique remember the words.

• Be Enthusiastic: Use a clear and cheerful voice when you say the words. Your enthusiasm will capture your bird's attention and make it more likely to want to mimic you.

3. Reward Vocalization

Positive reinforcement is essential in encouraging your caique to talk:

• Praise Your Bird: Whenever your caique tries to mimic a sound or word, immediately reward it with praise. Use a cheerful tone to show your excitement.

• Use Treats: Along with verbal praise, offer a small treat as a reward. This could be a piece of fruit or a favorite snack. Rewarding your caique will encourage it to keep trying to mimic sounds and words.

4. Create a Talking Environment

The environment around your caique can influence its ability to learn to talk:

• Play Recordings: Play recordings of other birds talking. Caiques often learn from listening to other birds, so hearing conversations can inspire your caique to start vocalizing.

• Engage in Conversations: Talk to other people near your caique. Your bird may become curious and want to join in the conversation. Talking around your caique creates a social environment that encourages vocalization.

5. Be Patient

Patience is crucial when teaching your caique to talk:

• Take Your Time: Remember that teaching your caique to talk can take a while. Some birds may learn quickly, while others need more time to catch on.

• Celebrate Small Successes: When your caique attempts to mimic a sound or word, celebrate its efforts, even if it is not perfect. Keeping the mood light and fun will motivate your bird to keep trying.

Additional Tips for Success

Here are some extra tips to help you teach your caique to talk:

1. Consistent Training Sessions

• Keep It Short: Try to keep your training sessions short, around 5 to 10 minutes. Caiques have short attention spans, so shorter sessions help keep them focused.

• Daily Practice: Try to practice a little every day. Consistent practice will help reinforce what your caique is learning.

2. Use Visual Aids

• Use Gestures: When you say a word, consider using hand gestures or pointing to objects related to the word. For example, when you say "apple," point to the apple or hold one up. This helps your caique connect the word with its meaning.

3. Make It Fun

• Incorporate Games: Turn the training sessions into fun games. For instance, you can reward your bird for mimicking words by playing a fun game afterward. This creates a positive association with learning.

4. Create a Bond

• Build Trust: Spend quality time with your caique outside of training sessions. The more your bird trusts you, the more likely it will want to engage and learn from you.

CHAPTER 4

How To Train Fun Tricks (Flips, And Spins)

Teaching your caique to perform tricks is a fun and rewarding experience. Not only does it show off your bird's intelligence, but it also strengthens the bond between you and your caique. Here, we'll go over some popular tricks, like flips and spins, and provide simple steps for teaching each one.

Teaching Flips

Flips are a fun trick that can impress your friends and family. Here's how to teach your caique to flip:

1. Start with the Step-Up Command:

i. Before teaching the flip, make sure your caique is comfortable stepping onto your hand. This helps your bird feel secure and ready to learn.

2. Introduce the Flip Motion:

i. Hold a treat in your hand.

ii. Gently guide your caique in a circular motion while holding the treat.

iii. Use a cue word like "flip" as you move the treat. The motion should encourage your caique to follow and roll over.

3. Reward the Movement:

i. If your caique attempts to follow the treat and starts to flip over, immediately reward it with the treat and praise. This helps your bird understand that flipping is a good behavior.

4. Practice:

i. Repeat this process several times during training sessions. The more your caique practices, the more it will associate the action with the cue word "flip."

Teaching Spins

Spins are another entertaining trick that is easy to teach. Follow these steps to help your caique learn to spin:

1. Get Your Bird's Attention:

i. Hold a treat in front of your caique's beak to capture its focus.

2. Guide the Spin:

i. Move the treat in a circular motion. Encourage your caique to follow the treat by using a cue word like "spin."

ii. It's important to keep the treat at the right distance to encourage your bird to move.

3. Reward for Success:

i. As soon as your caique completes the spin, reward it immediately with praise and the treat. This positive reinforcement encourages your bird to spin again in the future.

4. Repeat:

i. Keep practicing the spin during your training sessions. Over time, your caique will learn to spin on command without needing the treat as a guide.

Other Tricks

In addition to flips and spins, you can teach your caique other fun tricks, like waving or playing dead. Here are some tips for teaching these tricks:

1. Waving:

i. To teach your caique to wave, hold a treat in your hand and encourage your bird to lift its foot. Use a cue word like "wave."

ii. When it lifts its foot, reward it with a treat. Practice regularly until your caique associates the action with the cue.

2. Playing Dead:

i. For the "play dead" trick, gently guide your caique to lie on its side using a treat.

ii. Use a cue like "play dead" while encouraging this position. Reward your bird when it lies down.

Tips for Successful Training

• Use Positive Reinforcement: Always reward your caique with treats and praise for small successes. Positive reinforcement helps your bird learn faster and keeps it motivated.

• Keep Sessions Short: Caiques have short attention spans, so limit training sessions to about 5-10 minutes. Frequent, shorter sessions can be more effective than longer ones.

• End on a Positive Note: Always finish your training sessions with a success, even if it's just a simple task. Ending on a positive note helps your caique feel accomplished.

• Be Patient: Remember that every caique is different. Some birds may learn quickly, while others may need more time. Be patient and celebrate small achievements along the way.

• Have Fun: The most important part of training is to have fun! Enjoy the time you spend with your caique, and make the learning experience enjoyable for both of you.

Clicker Training For Caiques

Clicker training is a fun and effective way to teach your caique new behaviors and tricks. This method uses a small device called a clicker that makes a clicking sound to signal your bird when it has done something right. Here's a step-by-step guide on how to use clicker training with your caique.

Step 1: Get a Clicker

First, you need to get a clicker. You can find a clicker at a pet store or online. Choose one that is easy to press and makes a clear sound. The sound is important because it will be the signal your caique learns to associate with a reward.

Step 2: Introduce the Clicker

Before you start training, your caique needs to learn what the clicker means. Here's how to do this:

1. Click and Treat: Press the clicker to make a sound, and immediately give your caique a treat.

2. Repeat: Do this several times in a row. Each time you click, make sure to give a treat right after the sound. This helps your bird understand that the click means something good is coming.

Keep repeating this process until your caique starts to expect a treat after hearing the click. This connection between the sound and the reward is crucial for effective training.

Step 3: Use the Clicker in Training

Once your caique understands that the clicker means a treat is coming, you can start using it during training sessions. Here's how:

1. Mark the Behavior: As you teach your caique a new trick or behavior, use the clicker to mark the exact moment your bird does what you want. For example, if you are teaching your caique to spin, click the moment it completes

the spin.

2. Follow with a Treat: After clicking, immediately give your caique a treat. This way, your bird learns that it did something right when it hears the click.

3. Be Specific: The click should happen at the exact time your caique performs the desired action. This precision helps your bird connect the behavior with the reward.

Step 4: Gradually Fade the Treats

As your caique becomes more comfortable with the trick, you can start to reduce the number of treats you give. Here's how:

1. Less Frequent Treats: Instead of giving a treat every time you click, you can give a treat every second or third time. This helps your caique learn that it doesn't always get a treat but should still perform the behavior when it hears the click.

2. Keep Using the Clicker: Even as you reduce treats, continue using the clicker consistently. The click will remain a strong signal that your caique is doing the right thing.

3. Mix It Up: You can also mix in praise or affection instead of treats. For example, after clicking, you might say "good bird" and give a gentle scratch on the head. This way, your caique still gets positive reinforcement even when treats are less frequent.

Tips for Successful Clicker Training

• Be Patient: Clicker training takes time, so be patient with your caique. Every bird learns at its own pace, so celebrate small successes along the way.

• Keep Sessions Short: Limit training sessions to 5-10 minutes. Caiques have short attention spans, and shorter sessions will keep your bird engaged and focused.

• End on a High Note: Always try to end your training sessions with a successful behavior. This leaves your caique feeling accomplished and excited for the next session.

• Stay Consistent: Use the same cues and commands each time you train. Consistency helps your caique learn faster.

• Make It Fun: Keep the training sessions enjoyable for both you and your caique. Incorporate play and laughter to create a positive atmosphere.

CHAPTER 4

Problem Solving With Trick Training

Training your caique can be a fun and rewarding experience, but it can also come with some challenges. Understanding these challenges and knowing how to solve them can help you and your bird succeed in training. Here are some common problems you might face during training sessions and how to address them.

1. Inconsistent Responses

Sometimes, your caique may not respond reliably to the commands you've taught. This can be frustrating, but there are ways to fix it:

• Review the Training Process: Look back at how you've been training your bird. Make sure you are using the same commands and cues each time. Consistency is important for your caique to learn what you expect.

• Check the Environment: Sometimes distractions in the environment can make it hard for your caique to focus. Try training in a quiet room without too much noise or activity.

• Use High-Value Rewards: If your caique is not responding, it might not be motivated enough. Use treats that your bird really loves. This can help make training more exciting for them.

• Be Patient: If your caique still struggles, give it some time. Birds may have off days just like people do.

2. Boredom

Boredom can be a common issue in trick training. If your caique seems uninterested or stops participating, here's what you can do:

• Change the Routine: Mixing things up can help keep your caique engaged. Introduce new tricks or switch up the order of activities during your training sessions.

• Vary the Length of Sessions: If your training sessions are too long, your bird might lose interest. Keep sessions short, around 5-10 minutes, to keep your caique focused and excited.

• Incorporate Playtime: Include play breaks during training. Use toys or games that your caique enjoys to make the experience more enjoyable. After a short play session, return to training with renewed energy.

- Switch Locations: Sometimes a change of scenery can spark interest. Try training in different rooms or even outside, if it's safe. New environments can be stimulating for your bird.

3. Frustration

If your caique appears frustrated or anxious during training, it's important to address this feeling right away:

- Take a Break: If you notice signs of frustration, like fidgeting or squawking, stop the training session. Allow your bird to take a break and relax. Birds can get stressed, and a little time off can help.
- Keep Sessions Positive: Always end training on a positive note. If your caique successfully does something, even if it's small, give lots of praise and a treat. This builds confidence and makes training enjoyable.
- Be Patient: Understand that learning takes time. Some tricks may be harder for your caique than others. Give your bird the space it needs to process and learn at its own pace.

4. Over-Excitement

Caiques can sometimes get overly excited during training sessions, making it hard for them to focus. Here's how to handle that:

- Pause the Session: If your caique becomes too excited, it's best to take a short break. Calmly stop the training and give your bird a moment to settle down.
- Use Calm Commands: Speak to your caique in a soft and calm voice. This helps to soothe them and reminds them to be more relaxed.
- Reintroduce Training Gradually: Once your caique has calmed down, you can start the training session again. Start with simple commands or behaviors that your bird can easily accomplish.
- Monitor Your Energy: Your energy can influence your caique's behavior. If you're feeling energetic, try to calm your own demeanor before training. Keeping your energy level steady can help your bird remain focused.

Managing Training Expectations

Training your caique can be an exciting adventure, but it's important to manage your expectations as you engage in advanced training. Each bird is different, and understanding this can make the process smoother and more enjoyable. Here are some key points to consider when training your caique.

1. Individual Differences

Just like people, every caique has its own personality and learning style. Some caiques may quickly learn tricks and commands, while others may take longer to grasp the same concepts. It's essential to remember that this is normal.

- Recognize Unique Traits: Pay attention to your caique's individual quirks and strengths. Some birds may excel in vocal mimicry, while others might be better at physical tricks. Understanding these differences can help you tailor your training approach.

- Don't Compare: Avoid comparing your caique to others. Focus on your bird's progress rather than how it measures up to another caique. Each bird learns at its own pace, and that's perfectly okay.

2. Focus on Progress

Training can be challenging, especially when trying to teach more advanced tricks. Instead of focusing solely on mastering a trick, celebrate the small achievements along the way.

- Celebrate Small Wins: Acknowledge any progress your caique makes, even if it's just a small step toward the final trick. For example, if your caique starts to show interest in a new command, that's a victory worth celebrating.

- Keep a Positive Attitude: Every bit of progress contributes to your caique's learning journey. A positive mindset will help you and your bird stay motivated and enthusiastic about training.

3. Enjoy the Process

Training should be a fun experience for both you and your caique. If it becomes too stressful or serious, it may hinder your bird's ability to learn.

- Have Fun Together: Approach training sessions with a lighthearted attitude. Use games and playful activities to make the process enjoyable.

If both you and your caique are having fun, it will enhance the learning experience.

• Laugh Off Setbacks: Sometimes, your caique may not respond as you hoped or may even act silly during training. Instead of getting frustrated, try to see the humor in the situation. This will help create a positive atmosphere for both of you.

4. Be Patient

Advanced training takes time and patience. It's important to remember that birds are not like humans and may need more time to learn new tricks or commands.

• Consistent Practice: Regular, short training sessions are more effective than long, infrequent ones. This keeps your caique engaged without overwhelming it. Aim for about 5-10 minutes per session to maintain your bird's focus and interest.

• Repeat Often: Repetition is key to helping your caique learn. If a trick isn't mastered after a few tries, that's okay! Consistent practice will eventually lead to improvement.

5. Avoid Pressure

While having goals is important, putting too much pressure on your caique can lead to stress and frustration for both of you.

• Keep It Low-Key: Approach each training session without high expectations. Allow your caique to progress at its own pace. If it feels pressured, it may not respond well or may even shy away from training.

• Enjoy the Journey: Training is about building a bond with your caique. Focus on enjoying the time spent together rather than just the end results. This way, you'll create a strong relationship based on trust and fun.

5

Chapter 5

PLAYTIME AND ENRICHMENT

Importance Of Mental Stimulation For Caiques

Caiques are small, colorful parrots known for their playful and curious personalities. In the wild, they spend their time searching for food, climbing trees, and interacting with other birds in their flock. When kept as pets, caiques need similar experiences to keep their minds engaged and active. Just like people, birds need mental stimulation to stay happy and healthy. Here are some important reasons why mental stimulation is vital for caiques.

Prevents Boredom

One of the main reasons mental stimulation is important for caiques is that it helps prevent boredom. Birds that do not have enough activities to keep them busy can become bored and unhappy. When caiques get bored, they might start showing unwanted behaviors. For example, they may scream excessively, pluck their feathers, or become aggressive. These behaviors are signs that your bird is not mentally satisfied. By providing your caique with different activities and toys, you can keep its mind engaged and reduce the chances of boredom-related problems.

Enhances Learning

Mental stimulation also plays a crucial role in helping caiques learn and explore their environment. Just like humans, caiques are intelligent creatures that enjoy learning new things. Engaging your bird in various activities encourages it to use its brain. This can involve teaching your caique new tricks, solving puzzles, or exploring new toys. When caiques learn new skills, they become more confident and develop a greater sense of accomplishment. This learning process keeps their minds sharp and helps them adapt to new challenges in their environment.

Promotes Physical Health

Many activities that provide mental stimulation for caiques also involve physical movement. For example, playing with toys, climbing on perches, or participating in training sessions all require your bird to be active. This physical activity is essential for keeping your caique fit and healthy. Regular exercise helps prevent obesity, which can lead to various health issues in birds, such as heart disease and joint problems. By ensuring your caique has plenty of opportunities for physical activity, you are promoting its overall well-being.

Strengthens Bonding

Participating in play and enrichment activities with your caique can strengthen the bond between you and your bird. When you spend time together, engaging in fun activities, it creates a positive environment where your caique feels loved and secure. This bond is important for your bird's emotional health. A strong relationship can make your caique more trusting and affectionate toward you. Activities such as training, playing games, or simply spending time together can enhance this connection and lead to a happier, healthier bird.

Examples of Mental Stimulation Activities

To ensure your caique gets the mental stimulation it needs, you can incorporate a variety of activities into its daily routine. Here are some examples:

1. Interactive Toys: Provide toys that challenge your caique, such as puzzles that require it to figure out how to get treats. These toys can keep your bird

entertained and mentally engaged for hours.

2. Foraging Opportunities: Hide your caique's food in different locations around its cage or play area. This encourages it to search for food, simulating the foraging behavior it would experience in the wild.

3. Training Sessions: Spend time teaching your caique new tricks or commands. This not only stimulates its mind but also improves its behavior and strengthens your bond.

4. Varied Environments: Occasionally change the layout of your caique's cage or introduce new perches and climbing structures. This keeps your bird's environment interesting and encourages exploration.

5. Social Interaction: Caiques are social birds, so spend time interacting with them daily. Whether it's talking, playing, or simply being near them, your presence can provide much-needed mental stimulation.

6. Outdoor Time: If possible, allow your caique to enjoy some safe outdoor time. Fresh air and new sights and sounds can be exciting and enriching for your bird.

Creating A Daily Play Routine

Establishing a daily play routine is very important for your caique's mental and physical health. A structured schedule helps your bird understand when to expect playtime, making it easier for both of you to engage in fun activities together. A consistent routine can improve your caique's happiness and well-being. Here are some tips for creating a successful daily play routine.

Set a Consistent Time

The first step in creating a daily play routine is to choose a specific time each day for play and enrichment activities. You can select a time in the morning, afternoon, or evening—whatever works best for you and your caique. Consistency is key. When your bird knows when playtime will happen, it will feel more secure and relaxed. This structure can help your caique look forward to playtime and encourage it to engage in activities more eagerly.

Plan for Variety

To keep your caique interested and prevent boredom, plan for a variety of activities in your daily routine. Different types of play can include toys, games, training sessions, and foraging activities. Rotating the toys and activities regularly will keep things fresh and exciting for your bird. For example, you can have a few toys available one day and switch to different ones the next day. You could also try introducing new games or puzzles every week. The more variety you provide, the more engaged your caique will be.

Examples of Activities

Here are some ideas for fun activities to include in your routine:

• Toys: Choose interactive toys that challenge your caique, such as those that require your bird to solve puzzles to get treats.

• Games: Play games like fetch or hide-and-seek to stimulate your bird mentally and physically.

• Training: Spend time teaching your caique simple tricks, such as waving or spinning. Training is a great way to bond with your bird while providing mental stimulation.

Include Free Play

Another important aspect of your caique's play routine is allowing it time outside its cage for free play. Supervised free play is essential because it gives your bird the chance to explore, climb, and play at its own pace. You can create a safe play area where your caique can feel comfortable and have fun.

Safe Play Area

To set up a safe play area, consider the following:

• Location: Choose a space where your bird can play without any hazards, such as electrical cords or small objects it could swallow.

• Perches and Climbing Structures: Provide different perches, climbing toys, and safe branches for your caique to explore.

• Toys: Include a variety of toys to keep your caique engaged during free play.

Monitor Playtime Duration

When planning your play sessions, it's important to monitor the duration of each activity. Aim to keep structured play sessions to about 20 to 30 minutes. Shorter sessions can be more effective in maintaining your bird's attention and enthusiasm. If you notice your caique losing interest, it may be time to switch activities or take a break. This approach helps prevent overstimulation and keeps playtime enjoyable for your bird.

Observe Your Caique

Every caique is different, and it's essential to observe your bird's preferences to create a play routine that suits its needs. Some caiques may enjoy physical games that involve climbing and moving around, while others may prefer solving puzzles or foraging for treats.

Adjusting the Routine

Pay close attention to your caique's reactions during playtime. If your bird seems excited about a particular toy or activity, make sure to include it regularly in your routine. Conversely, if it shows little interest in something, consider removing it and trying different activities. This flexibility will help you create a routine that keeps your caique happy and engaged.

DIY Toys And Activities

One of the best ways to keep your caique happy and engaged is by providing DIY toys and activities. Homemade toys are not only more cost-effective than store-bought ones, but they can also be customized to fit your bird's specific interests and preferences. Making toys for your caique can be a fun and creative way to bond with your pet while ensuring it has plenty of enrichment. Here are some simple and enjoyable DIY toy ideas and activities to try with your caique.

1. Paper Rolls

One easy and fun DIY toy you can create is a paper roll toy. You can use empty toilet paper or paper towel rolls to make these. Here's how:

• What You Need: Empty toilet paper or paper towel rolls, treats, and shredded paper or crumpled tissue.

• How to Make It: Take an empty roll and fill it with your caique's favorite treats, or stuff it with shredded paper. You can also place some shredded paper at the ends to keep the treats from falling out.

• Why It's Fun: Your caique will love foraging through the roll to find the hidden goodies. It mimics the natural behavior of searching for food in the wild, providing both mental stimulation and entertainment.

2. Birdie Kabobs

Another great DIY activity is creating birdie kabobs. This is a fun and interactive snack that your caique will enjoy.

• What You Need: Skewers or untreated wooden dowels, and a variety of fruits, vegetables, and bird-safe treats (like nuts or seeds).

• How to Make It: Thread pieces of fruits and vegetables onto the skewer. You can alternate between different items for variety, making it colorful and appealing. Hang the kabob in your caique's cage.

• Why It's Fun: This not only provides a tasty treat but also encourages your caique to work for its food, which is stimulating and enjoyable.

3. Shreddable Toys

Caiques love to chew and shred, so shreddable toys are a fantastic option. These toys can be made from safe materials that allow your bird to satisfy its natural chewing instincts.

• What You Need: Untreated wood, cardboard, and paper. Avoid any materials that have been treated with chemicals.

• How to Make It: You can create simple toys by cutting cardboard into shapes, or you can tie pieces of paper or soft wood together to make a toy that your caique can shred.

• Why It's Fun: The act of tearing and shredding provides a great outlet for your bird's energy and helps keep its beak healthy.

4. Puzzle Toys

Creating puzzle toys is a great way to challenge your caique's problem-solving skills. These toys can provide hours of entertainment.

• What You Need: A cardboard box, scissors, and your caique's favorite treats.

• How to Make It: Cut small holes in the box and place treats inside. Make sure the holes are just big enough for your caique to reach in and grab the treats but not so big that the treats fall out easily.

• Why It's Fun: Your caique will have to figure out how to reach the treats, which promotes mental engagement and keeps it occupied. It's a rewarding challenge for your bird!

5. Hanging Toys

Hanging toys can add excitement to your caique's cage environment and encourage exploration.

• What You Need: String or rope, various materials like fabric scraps, bells, beads, or colorful paper.

• How to Make It: Use the string or rope to create hanging toys by tying different materials together. You can include bells for auditory stimulation and colorful items to attract your bird's attention.

• Why It's Fun: Hanging toys encourage climbing and swinging, which are natural behaviors for caiques. The different textures and sounds will keep your bird curious and entertained.

Foraging Games And Puzzle Feeders

Foraging is a natural and important behavior for caiques. In the wild, these birds spend a lot of time searching for food, which keeps their minds sharp and their bodies active. To replicate this natural behavior at home, it's essential to provide foraging opportunities that enrich their environment. Foraging games and puzzle feeders not only challenge your caique's mind but also encourage it to engage in instinctual behaviors. Here are some fun ideas to incorporate foraging activities into your caique's daily routine.

1. Foraging Baskets

One simple and engaging activity is creating foraging baskets. This is an excellent way to stimulate your caique's natural foraging instincts.

• What You Need: A small basket, crumpled paper, hay, or shredded newspaper, and some of your caique's favorite treats.

• How to Make It: Fill the basket with crumpled paper, hay, or shredded newspaper. Make sure the materials are safe for your bird to dig through. Then, hide some treats within the basket. You can use nuts, seeds, or small pieces of fruit.

• Why It's Fun: Your caique will enjoy digging through the materials to find the hidden treats. This activity keeps your bird engaged and allows it to express its natural foraging behavior.

2. Puzzle Feeders

Puzzle feeders are another fantastic way to provide mental stimulation for your caique. These feeders are designed to require your bird to solve a challenge in order to access its food.

• What You Need: A commercially available puzzle feeder or you can make your own using a regular feeder.

• How to Use It: Fill the puzzle feeder with your caique's food or treats. The feeder might have sliding doors, hidden compartments, or other mechanisms that require your bird to figure out how to get to the food.

• Why It's Fun: By working to access the food, your caique engages in problem-solving and critical thinking. This not only makes mealtime more exciting but also prolongs it, allowing your bird to feel accomplished after successfully retrieving its food.

3. Foraging Boards

Creating a foraging board is another great way to encourage your caique to forage for its food.

• What You Need: A wooden board, small toys, paper, or natural elements like leaves or branches. You can also use safe items you find at home.

• How to Make It: Attach various items to the board using glue or screws. Make sure they are securely fastened so that your caique cannot pull them off easily. Hide some treats in between the items, making them less visible.

• Why It's Fun: Your caique will have to search through the board to find the treats hidden among the items. This activity stimulates your bird's natural curiosity and encourages it to explore its environment.

4. Hiding Treats

Another simple way to encourage foraging is by hiding treats around your caique's play area or cage.

• What You Need: Small treats or pellets that your caique enjoys.

• How to Do It: Scatter small treats throughout your bird's play area or within its cage. You can hide them in different places, such as under perches, inside toys, or between climbing structures.

• Why It's Fun: This activity encourages exploration and rewards your caique for foraging. Your bird will have fun searching for the treats, and it will get some exercise while doing so.

Benefits of Foraging Activities

Incorporating foraging games and puzzle feeders into your caique's daily routine offers numerous benefits:

- Mental Stimulation: Foraging activities keep your bird's mind active and engaged, helping to prevent boredom and related behavioral problems.
- Physical Exercise: Searching for food requires movement, which helps keep your caique physically fit and healthy.
- Natural Behaviors: These activities mimic the natural behaviors of birds in the wild, allowing your caique to express its instincts and feel more fulfilled.
- Bonding Time: Engaging in foraging activities together can strengthen the bond between you and your caique, creating a more positive environment for both of you.

Interactive Play With Your Caique

Interactive playtime is crucial for developing a strong bond with your caique and keeping it mentally stimulated. Engaging in fun activities together can help your bird feel loved and secure while providing essential exercise and mental challenges. Here are some enjoyable interactive play ideas you can try with your caique.

1. Fetch

A classic game that many birds enjoy is fetch. This game is simple and can be a great way to engage your caique's playful side.

- What You Need: A small, lightweight ball or toy that is safe for your caique to handle.
- How to Play: Start by tossing the toy a short distance away. Encourage your caique to go after it. When your bird picks up the toy, call it back to you. If your caique brings the toy back, reward it with praise or a small treat.
- Why It's Fun: This game mimics natural hunting behaviors and allows your caique to use its instincts. Plus, it creates a fun and interactive way for your bird to bond with you.

2. Tug-of-War

Another fun interactive activity is a gentle game of tug-of-war. This game allows your caique to engage with you in a playful way.

• What You Need: A bird-safe rope or a soft toy that is safe for chewing.

• How to Play: Hold one end of the rope or toy, and allow your caique to grab the other end with its beak. Gently pull on the toy, encouraging your bird to pull back. Keep the game light and controlled.

• Why It's Fun: Tug-of-war allows your caique to engage its strength and energy in a safe manner. Just make sure the game remains friendly and that you don't pull too hard. It should be a fun and cooperative activity for both of you!

3. Obstacle Course

Creating a mini obstacle course is another exciting way to interact with your caique. This activity promotes physical exercise while challenging your bird mentally.

• What You Need: Various items like perches, toys, tunnels, or anything that can serve as obstacles.

• How to Set It Up: Arrange the items in a way that creates a path for your caique to navigate. You can set up a few different routes or challenges, depending on your available space and your bird's abilities.

• How to Play: Encourage your caique to explore the course. Use treats or praise as motivation to complete each section. You can reward your bird for navigating through the obstacles successfully.

• Why It's Fun: An obstacle course allows your caique to use its problem-solving skills while providing physical activity. Watching your bird figure out how to navigate the course can be very entertaining!

4. Dance Party

Many caiques enjoy music, so having a dance party can be a delightful way to interact with your bird.

• What You Need: Some fun music that you both enjoy!

• How to Play: Put on some upbeat music and start moving to the beat. Encourage your caique to dance along with you. You might notice your bird bobbing its head or moving its feet to the rhythm.

• Why It's Fun: Dancing can be a joyful experience for both you and your caique. It creates a lively atmosphere and can make your bird feel more relaxed and happy. Plus, your bird may even mimic some of your movements!

5. Interactive Training

Incorporating training sessions into your playtime is another excellent way to keep your caique mentally engaged while having fun together.

• What You Need: Treats that your caique enjoys, and maybe some training tools like a clicker if you choose to use one.

• How to Train: Choose a trick or command you want to teach your caique, such as "step up," "spin," or "wave." Start with simple commands and use positive reinforcement. Reward your bird with treats or praise every time it follows your command.

• Why It's Fun: Training sessions can be stimulating and rewarding for both you and your caique. They not only teach your bird new skills but also strengthen your bond. Plus, as your caique learns new tricks, you'll both feel a sense of accomplishment!

UNDERSTANDING CAIQUE BEHAVIOR

Exploring The Playful Nature Of Caiques

Caiques are often called the clowns of the parrot world. This nickname comes from their playful and mischievous behavior. These lively birds are highly active and need both mental and physical stimulation to stay happy and healthy. In this section, we'll explore the various aspects of caiques' playful nature, including their love for play, curiosity, ability to mimic sounds, and their need for social interaction.

1. Playfulness

Caiques are extremely playful birds. They enjoy engaging with various toys and are often seen swinging, climbing, and exploring their surroundings. Here are some ways they express their playfulness:

• Toys: Caiques love to play with a variety of toys. They often enjoy chewable toys, ropes, and puzzles that challenge their minds. When provided with different kinds of toys, they can spend hours playing, climbing, and swinging, which keeps them physically active and mentally stimulated.

• Games: These birds are known for their love of games. They might play simple games like toss-and-catch with their owners or chase each other around. Caiques also enjoy hide-and-seek, where they hide behind objects or under covers before popping out to surprise you!

• Exploring: Their playful nature drives them to explore their environment. You might find your caique climbing up curtains, perching on top of furniture, or even rummaging through items in search of hidden treasures.

2. Curiosity

Caiques are naturally curious creatures. They love to investigate new objects or changes in their surroundings, which often leads to playful interactions. Here's how their curiosity manifests:

• Investigation: When you introduce a new toy or object into their environment, you'll likely see your caique examining it closely. They may tilt their heads, poke at it, or even try to climb on it to get a better look. This exploration is part of their playful behavior, as they learn about their world through tactile and visual experiences.

• New Experiences: Caiques are always eager to explore new areas of your home. They enjoy being taken to different rooms or introduced to new sights and sounds. Whether it's a new plant, a shiny object, or even a new pet, they will quickly investigate it. This curiosity keeps them engaged and stimulated.

3. Mimicking

Another fascinating aspect of caiques' playful nature is their ability to mimic sounds and behaviors. This talent adds to their entertaining personality in several ways:

• Imitating Sounds: Caiques can mimic a variety of sounds, from household noises to human speech. They might imitate the sound of a ringing phone, a microwave beep, or even laughter. This ability not only showcases their playful side but also adds to the fun of having them around.

• Playful Antics: Their mimicking often leads to playful antics. For example, if you have other pets, your caique might try to imitate their sounds or behaviors, which can be both amusing and heartwarming. This mimicking can also include trying to copy your actions, like dancing or waving, which makes for delightful interactions.

4. Social Interaction

Caiques are highly social birds and thrive on interaction with their owners and other birds. Their need for social interaction contributes significantly to their playful nature:

- Bonding with Owners: Caiques enjoy spending time with their owners and often seek attention. They might engage in playful behavior to grab your attention, such as climbing on you, playfully nipping at your fingers, or performing tricks. This social interaction strengthens the bond between you and your bird.

- Family Activities: These birds love being part of family activities. They often become the center of attention with their playful antics. Whether you're watching TV, cooking, or simply hanging out, your caique will likely want to join in the fun. Their playful nature makes them entertaining companions, as they are always ready to add some joy and laughter to your day.

Aggression And Hormonal Changes

Caiques are known for their playful and friendly nature, but they can sometimes show aggressive behavior. Understanding why this happens is important for addressing any aggression effectively, especially during hormonal changes. This section will explain the main causes of aggression in caiques, including hormonal changes, mating behavior, resource guarding, and fear or stress.

1. Hormonal Changes

Like many birds, caiques experience hormonal changes, particularly during specific seasons. These hormonal shifts usually occur in spring and fall. Here's how these changes can affect their behavior:

- Increased Aggression: During hormonal seasons, caiques may become more aggressive. This is especially true for male caiques, who may feel more territorial. They might try to defend their space more vigorously during this time, leading to more aggressive actions towards perceived threats.

- Territorial Behavior: As hormones surge, caiques may feel the need to establish and defend their territory. This can result in aggressive behaviors such as lunging, biting, or even vocalizing loudly to warn others away. Understanding this behavior is key to managing it effectively.

2. Mating Behavior

During periods of heightened hormones, caiques may also exhibit mating behaviors. This can include various actions that may come off as aggressive, such as:

• Chasing: Caiques may chase other birds or even their owners during mating season. This behavior can be playful, but it can also become aggressive if the bird feels threatened or challenged.

• Biting: Some caiques may resort to biting during hormonal peaks. This is often directed at perceived rivals or threats. While this behavior is natural for caiques, it can be concerning for owners, who may not understand why their usually friendly bird is acting out.

• Displaying Aggression: Mating behaviors can include puffing up feathers, displaying brightly colored markings, and making loud calls. While these actions are part of their natural behavior, they can come off as aggressive and intimidating.

3. Resource Guarding

Another common cause of aggression in caiques is resource guarding. This behavior occurs when caiques become possessive over items they consider valuable, such as:

• Food: Caiques may defend their food bowls, becoming aggressive if they feel someone is trying to take their food away. This can include lunging or biting if they perceive a threat to their meal.

• Toys: Toys are another resource that caiques may guard. If they feel someone is trying to take their favorite toy or if another bird approaches their toy, they may react aggressively to protect it.

• Cage: Caiques often view their cage as their personal space. If they feel threatened or challenged when someone approaches their cage, they may exhibit aggressive behaviors to defend their territory.

4. Fear or Stress

Aggression in caiques can also arise from fear or stress. Various factors can trigger these feelings, including:

• Environmental Changes: Sudden changes in their environment, such as moving to a new home, rearranging furniture, or introducing new pets, can make caiques feel insecure and stressed. This stress can lead to aggressive behaviors as they try to cope with the changes.

• Loud Noises: Caiques are sensitive to loud noises, such as thunder, fireworks, or even vacuum cleaners. These sounds can startle them, causing fear. If a caique feels frightened, it may react aggressively as a defense mechanism.

• Unfamiliar People or Pets: The presence of strangers or unfamiliar animals can also trigger fear in caiques. If they feel threatened, they may resort to aggressive behavior to protect themselves.

Managing Aggression in Caiques

Understanding the causes of aggression in caiques is the first step in managing it effectively. Here are some tips to help:

1. Identify Triggers: Pay attention to when aggressive behaviors occur. Identifying the triggers can help you understand the underlying causes.

2. Create a Safe Space: Make sure your caique has a safe and secure environment. This can help reduce stress and fear, which may, in turn, reduce aggressive behavior.

3. Positive Reinforcement: Use positive reinforcement techniques to reward calm behavior. This can include treats, praise, or toys when your caique behaves well.

4. Minimize Stress: Try to keep your caique's environment stable and predictable. Reducing loud noises and minimizing sudden changes can help your bird feel more secure.

5. Consult an Expert: If aggressive behavior persists or worsens, consider consulting an avian veterinarian or a bird behaviorist. They can provide tailored advice and support for managing aggression.

Vocalization: Chirps, Whistles, And Calls

Caiques are vocal birds that communicate using a wide range of sounds. Understanding these vocalizations can help you better understand what your caique is feeling and what it needs. In this section, we will explore the different sounds caiques make, including chirps, whistles, calls, and vocalizations during play.

1. Chirps

Caiques often chirp, and this is one of their most common vocalizations. Here's what you need to know about their chirping:

• Happy Sounds: When caiques chirp, it is usually a sign that they are happy or excited. These cheerful, light sounds indicate that your bird is content and enjoying its surroundings. For example, if you hear your caique chirping while you are playing with it or when it sees you after being away, it is likely expressing joy.

• Engagement: Chirping is also a way for caiques to engage with their environment. They might chirp when they are exploring new toys or when they see something interesting outside the window. This vocalization shows that they are alert and curious.

• Communication: Chirping can serve as a form of communication between caiques. If you have more than one bird, they may chirp to each other, creating a lively atmosphere. It is their way of interacting and bonding with each other.

2. Whistles

Caiques are famous for their impressive whistling abilities. Here's how whistling fits into their communication:

• Mimicking Sounds: Caiques love to mimic sounds they hear around them. They may pick up tunes from songs you play, sounds from television shows, or even other animals' calls. When they whistle these tunes, it shows that they are playful and have a knack for imitation.

• Joyful Expression: Whistling is often a sign of playfulness and joy in caiques. If you hear your caique whistling a happy tune, it likely means it is feeling good and having fun. This joyful whistling can brighten your day and add to the cheerful atmosphere in your home.

- Engagement with Owners: Caiques may also whistle to get your attention or to invite you to play. If your bird whistles when you enter the room or while you are nearby, it is trying to engage with you and share its excitement.

3. Calls

In addition to chirps and whistles, caiques can produce louder calls. These calls can serve several purposes:

- Seeking Attention: Caiques often call out loudly when they want attention. If your caique is calling, it might be trying to communicate that it wants to play, be petted, or simply interact with you. This call can be a way of saying, "Hey, notice me!"
- Communication with Other Birds: If you have multiple caiques or other birds, loud calls can be a way to communicate with each other. This is especially true if they are separated or in different rooms. They may call out to maintain contact or to signal that they are nearby.
- Reassurance: Caiques may also use loud calls to seek reassurance from their owners. If your caique feels uncertain or anxious, it might call out for comfort. Responding to these calls can help your bird feel more secure and connected to you.

4. Vocalizing During Play

Caiques can become particularly vocal during playtime. Their sounds during play can indicate their mood and energy level:

- Excitement: When caiques are playing, they often express their excitement through various vocalizations. You might hear a mix of chirps, whistles, and calls as they engage in fun activities. This vocalization adds to the playful atmosphere and shows that they are enjoying themselves.
- Different Sounds: Pay attention to the different sounds your caique makes while playing. Each sound may have its meaning. For example, quick, high-pitched chirps may indicate that your caique is very excited, while softer, lower sounds might mean it is feeling more relaxed and content.
- Expressing Emotions: The way your caique vocalizes during play can give you clues about its emotions. If it is energetic and happy, you will likely hear more lively sounds. On the other hand, if your caique seems frustrated or bored, it might make less noise or have a different tone in its vocalizations.

Caique Quirks And Unique Behaviors

Caiques are known for their lively personalities and unique behaviors that make them delightful pets. Their playful and sometimes silly actions can bring joy to your home. In this section, we will explore some common quirks and behaviors that caiques display, including bouncing, head bobbing, chewing and destruction, and their bathing rituals.

1. Bouncing

One of the most charming behaviors of caiques is their bouncing. Here's what you should know about this playful quirk:

• Excitement Indicator: Caiques often bounce up and down when they are excited or happy. This energetic movement usually occurs when they see their favorite toy, when you come home, or when they are about to play. The bouncing is a clear sign that your bird is feeling good and is ready to engage with you or its surroundings.

• Playful Nature: This bouncing behavior reflects their playful nature. Caiques are very active birds, and bouncing is one of the ways they express their joy. You might notice that your caique bounces more when it's in a playful mood, which can encourage you to join in on the fun.

• Encouraging Interaction: When your caique bounces, it's a great opportunity to interact with it. You can respond to this behavior by offering toys or initiating playtime, making it a bonding experience for both of you.

2. Head Bobbing

Head bobbing is another common behavior seen in caiques. Here's what it signifies:

• Request for Attention: Caiques often bob their heads up and down when they want attention or interaction. If your caique starts head bobbing, it could be signaling that it wants to play with you or simply wishes to be noticed. This behavior is a way for them to communicate their desire for engagement.

• Excitement and Happiness: Head bobbing can also indicate excitement. If your caique is feeling playful or happy, you might see it bobbing its head along with its bouncing. This behavior can be especially cute and is a clear sign that your bird is in a good mood.

- Social Behavior: Head bobbing is a social behavior that caiques use to interact with their owners and other birds. It shows their interest and willingness to connect with others. When you see your caique bobbing its head, it's a great time to respond and engage with it.

3. Chewing and Destruction

Caiques are natural chewers, and this behavior can lead to some amusing, if not frustrating, moments. Here's what to know:

- Natural Chewing Instinct: Caiques have a strong instinct to chew, which is important for their mental and physical health. Chewing helps keep their beaks healthy and can also relieve boredom. However, if they don't have enough appropriate toys, they may resort to chewing on furniture or other household items.

- Destructive Behavior: If your caique doesn't have enough toys to chew on, it may start engaging in destructive behaviors. This can include tearing up paper, chewing on wood furniture, or pulling at curtains. To prevent this, it's essential to provide a variety of safe, durable toys for your caique to chew on.

- Providing Appropriate Toys: Offering your caique plenty of chewable toys, such as wooden blocks, cardboard, and bird-safe rope, can help redirect its chewing behavior. This will satisfy its natural instincts and keep your home safe from destruction. Regularly rotating and introducing new toys can also keep your caique engaged and entertained.

4. Bathing Rituals

Many caiques love to bathe, and this behavior is both natural and fun. Here's what to know about their bathing rituals:

- Enjoyment of Water: Caiques often enjoy splashing around in water, whether it's in a shallow dish or through misting. This behavior is a fun activity for them and helps keep their feathers clean. You might notice your caique getting excited when it sees a bath setup.

- Misting and Shallow Dishes: You can encourage your caique to bathe by providing a shallow dish of water or misting it with a spray bottle. Many caiques will happily splash and play in the water, which can be a delightful sight. This bathing ritual allows them to express their playful nature and enjoy a refreshing activity.

- Health Benefits: Bathing is also beneficial for caiques' health. It helps keep their feathers clean and can aid in regulating their body temperature. Regular bathing can also prevent skin issues and promote a healthy, shiny coat.

How To Deal With Behavioral Challenges

Owning a caique can be a joyful experience, but sometimes you may encounter behavioral challenges. Understanding how to handle these challenges effectively can help create a happier and healthier environment for both you and your caique. Below are some helpful tips for dealing with common behavioral issues, such as biting, chewing, and aggression.

1. Redirect Negative Behavior

One of the most effective strategies for managing unwanted behaviors is to redirect your caique's attention. Here's how to do it:

- Identify Undesirable Behaviors: If your caique starts biting or chewing on furniture, it's important to recognize these negative behaviors early on. Being aware of what your caique is doing can help you intervene before the behavior escalates.

- Offer Appropriate Alternatives: When you see your caique engaging in undesirable behavior, quickly redirect its attention to a suitable toy or activity. For example, if your bird is chewing on your furniture, gently guide it towards a chew toy that is designed for birds. This gives your caique something acceptable to focus on instead.

- Positive Reinforcement: When your caique engages with the appropriate toy or activity, provide positive reinforcement. You can do this by offering praise, petting, or even a small treat. This encourages your caique to continue engaging with the right items and helps it learn which behaviors are acceptable.

2. Establish Boundaries

Setting clear boundaries is crucial for teaching your caique what behaviors are acceptable. Here's how to establish those boundaries:

- Clear Expectations: Make sure your caique understands the rules. For example, if biting is not acceptable, consistently enforce this rule every time it happens.

• Calm Time-Outs: If your caique bites or acts aggressively, calmly remove it from the situation and give it a time-out. This doesn't mean you are punishing your bird; rather, it helps it understand that such behavior is not acceptable. Time-outs can last a few minutes, allowing your caique to calm down and reflect on its actions.

• Consistency is Key: Consistency is crucial when establishing boundaries. Make sure all family members follow the same rules regarding your caique's behavior. This helps reinforce the lessons your bird is learning.

3. Provide Enrichment

Caiques are active, intelligent birds that require plenty of mental and physical stimulation. Here's how to ensure your caique has enough enrichment:

• Variety of Toys: Offer a range of toys that cater to your caique's natural instincts, such as chewing, climbing, and foraging. Toys made of different materials, textures, and colors can keep your bird engaged.

• Rotating Toys: Regularly rotate your caique's toys to keep things fresh and interesting. This prevents boredom and encourages your bird to explore new activities. A toy that may have been ignored for weeks can become exciting again when reintroduced.

• Scheduled Playtime: Create a daily routine that includes playtime. Allowing your caique time outside its cage to play can help reduce boredom-related behaviors. You can set up a safe play area with climbing structures, toys, and foraging activities to stimulate your bird's mind.

4. Understand Triggers

Every caique is unique, and understanding what triggers your bird's negative behavior is essential for addressing those issues. Here's how to recognize and manage triggers:

• Observe Behavior: Take note of when your caique exhibits unwanted behaviors. Is it during specific times of day, in response to certain noises, or when there are unfamiliar people around? Keeping a journal can help you track these patterns.

• Minimize Stress: Once you identify the triggers, try to minimize your caique's exposure to these stressors. For instance, if loud noises cause anxiety, create a quiet space for your bird where it can feel safe and secure.

• Gradual Exposure: If certain stimuli are unavoidable, consider gradual exposure. Allow your caique to get used to these triggers slowly. Start by exposing it to the stimulus at a low intensity and gradually increase it as your bird becomes more comfortable.

5. Seek Professional Help

If you find that you're struggling with your caique's behavior despite your best efforts, don't hesitate to seek help. Here are some options:

• Avian Veterinarian: An avian veterinarian can assess your bird's health and ensure that there are no underlying medical issues contributing to its behavior. Sometimes, health problems can manifest as aggression or other unwanted behaviors.

• Bird Behaviorist: An experienced bird behaviorist specializes in understanding avian behavior. They can provide valuable insights and personalized strategies to help manage your caique's challenges effectively.

• Support and Resources: Consider joining online forums or local bird clubs where you can share experiences and learn from other caique owners. Having a support network can provide encouragement and additional resources for managing behavioral challenges.

6

Chapter 6

SOCIALIZING YOUR CAIQUE

Introducing Your Caique To Other Pets

Introducing your caique to other pets can be a rewarding experience, but it's essential to do it carefully and thoughtfully. By following some straightforward steps, you can help ensure that everyone gets along well. Here's a guide to making the introduction process smooth and safe for your caique and your other pets.

1. Preparation

Before you begin the introduction process, you need to prepare your home. Start by creating a safe and quiet space for your caique. This space should be somewhere it can retreat to if it feels overwhelmed or scared. It's vital that your caique feels secure in its environment.

Next, introduce the idea of having a bird around to your other pets. If you have dogs or cats, allow them to see your caique from a distance. This way, they can get used to its presence without feeling threatened. You might want to hold your caique in a safe place, like a cage or a carrier, while the other pets observe it. This initial step helps all pets become familiar with each other gradually.

2. Gradual Introduction

Once your pets are somewhat accustomed to each other's presence, you can start the gradual introduction. Begin with short, supervised meetings. Place your caique in its secure cage or carrier and allow your other pets to approach it. Keep the first meetings brief to reduce any stress.

During these introductions, watch closely for any signs of aggression or anxiety. If you notice that any of your pets are getting upset or acting aggressively, separate them immediately and try again later. It's important to take things slow. Rushing the process can lead to fear or aggression, which can be dangerous for everyone involved.

3. Positive Reinforcement

Using positive reinforcement is a great way to encourage good behavior during the introductions. When your caique and your other pets are calm around each other, offer them treats and praise. This helps them associate each other's presence with positive experiences. For example, if your dog sits calmly near the cage, give it a treat. If your caique is quiet and relaxed, reward it as well.

By reinforcing good behavior, you can help your pets learn that being around each other is a positive thing. Consistency is key—try to reward them every time they behave well during interactions.

4. Supervised Interactions

As your pets become more comfortable with each other, you can start allowing them to interact more closely. Always supervise these interactions to ensure safety. For instance, you can let your caique out of its cage for short periods while keeping an eye on it around the other pets.

Be alert for any signs of stress or aggression. If you see any negative behavior, such as your dog barking excessively or your cat hissing, separate the pets right away. It's crucial to be ready to intervene if necessary. The goal is to create a safe environment where all your pets can feel secure and comfortable.

5. Regular Check-Ins

Even after the initial introductions, it's essential to continue monitoring your pets' interactions. Keep an eye on how they behave around each other over the following days and weeks. Gradually, they should start building a positive relationship, but you must remain vigilant, especially in the early stages.

If you notice any issues or if one of your pets seems stressed, don't hesitate to separate them again and revisit the previous steps. This might mean going back to short, supervised meetings or reinforcing positive behavior with treats.

How Caiques Interact With Other Birds

Caiques are known for their social nature and can interact well with other birds. However, the way they connect with other species depends on the temperament of those birds and how well they have been socialized. Understanding these interactions is essential to ensure a safe and happy environment for all your feathered friends. Here's what you need to know about how caiques interact with other birds.

1. Social Nature

Caiques are naturally social creatures. In the wild, they live in flocks and thrive on social interactions. This playful nature carries over into captivity, where caiques enjoy the company of other birds. They engage in various fun activities, such as chasing, playing games, and even mimicking sounds.

When caiques play with other birds, it can be a delightful experience for both species. Their energetic antics can provide entertainment and enrichment, making life more enjoyable for all the birds involved. Social interaction is crucial for caiques as it helps them stay mentally and physically stimulated, leading to a happier and healthier life.

2. Choosing Companions

When introducing your caique to other birds, it's important to choose companions wisely. Not all bird species will get along, and the temperament of the other bird plays a significant role. Caiques are generally friendly and playful, but they can be vulnerable to more aggressive or territorial species.

If you choose a bird that is more dominant or aggressive, it may stress your caique or lead to fights. Birds that are too shy may also not interact well with a caique, which could result in isolation for the less social bird. Look for species that have similar social needs and temperaments. For instance, other parrot species or friendly, social birds may be better companions for a caique.

3. Supervised Playtime

Safety is a priority when allowing your caique to interact with other birds. Always supervise these interactions closely. Watch for any signs of aggression or stress, such as loud squawking, flapping wings, or puffed-up feathers. These behaviors can indicate discomfort or the possibility of a conflict.

If one of the birds seems uncomfortable or scared, it's best to separate them immediately. Forcing interactions when one bird is not ready can lead to negative experiences and potential injury. It's crucial to create a positive environment for both birds. Supervision will help you intervene quickly if any issues arise, allowing you to keep all your birds safe.

4. Encouraging Interaction

If you have multiple birds, you can encourage interaction by placing their cages near each other. This setup allows the birds to see and hear each other without direct contact. Gradually, they can become accustomed to each other's presence. This method helps build familiarity and reduces the chances of aggression when you eventually introduce them more closely.

Make sure to monitor their behavior during this time. Observe how they react to each other; are they curious, indifferent, or aggressive? Positive interactions through the cage can lay the groundwork for a successful introduction later on.

5. Gradual Introductions

When it's time to introduce your caique to another bird more directly, do it gradually. Start with short visits in a neutral space, where neither bird feels territorial. Keep the initial meetings brief, allowing them to explore each other's presence without becoming overwhelmed.

As they become more comfortable, you can gradually increase the time they spend together. Pay attention to their body language; if both birds seem relaxed and playful, you can continue the interaction. However, if you notice any signs of stress or aggression, it's best to take a step back and allow them to acclimate further.

CHAPTER 6

Managing Multi-Pet Households

Having multiple pets can be a wonderful and fulfilling experience, but it also brings its own set of challenges. If you have a caique along with other pets, it's essential to create a harmonious environment for everyone. Here are some helpful tips for managing a household with a caique and other animals.

1. Creating Safe Spaces

One of the first steps to managing a multi-pet household is to create safe spaces for each pet. Every animal needs a place where they can retreat if they feel threatened or stressed. For your caique, this could be a quiet area in a separate room or a designated spot in its cage.

Make sure that this space is free from other pets and distractions, allowing your caique to feel secure. Providing a safe space is crucial for reducing stress and anxiety, especially during the adjustment period when all pets are getting used to each other.

2. Supervised Interactions

When introducing your caique to other pets, it's vital to supervise their interactions, especially in the beginning. Closely monitor their behavior during these meetings. Look for any signs of aggression, stress, or discomfort.

For example, if your dog shows too much interest in the caique, or if your caique appears frightened, it's essential to step in immediately. This supervision allows you to intervene quickly if things start to escalate, ensuring that all pets remain safe and comfortable.

As they get more accustomed to each other, you can gradually allow for less supervised interactions. However, it's best to maintain a watchful eye during their early encounters to build a positive relationship.

3. Routine and Consistency

Establishing a routine is vital for the well-being of all your pets. Create a consistent schedule for feeding, playtime, and other daily activities that includes everyone.

For example, feed your caique and other pets at the same time each day. This consistency helps your pets understand what to expect, making them feel more secure. When pets know when they will be fed or played with, it reduces anxiety and creates a calm atmosphere in your home.

Having a routine also helps you manage your time effectively. You can plan activities that include all your pets, ensuring that each one gets the attention and care they need.

4. Training

Training is an essential aspect of managing a multi-pet household, especially for your dogs. It's crucial to teach them how to behave gently around your caique. Commands such as "leave it" or "gentle" can be very helpful in preventing accidents and ensuring that interactions remain safe.

When your dog exhibits calm behavior around the caique, reward them with treats and praise. This positive reinforcement encourages good behavior and helps your dog understand how to interact appropriately with your caique.

It's also important to train your caique. Teaching it to respond to commands can help you manage interactions better. For example, teaching your caique to go to its safe space on command can be useful when other pets are around.

5. Consult Professionals

If you find it challenging to manage the dynamics of a multi-pet household, don't hesitate to seek help. Consulting a veterinarian or a professional animal behaviorist can provide valuable insights and strategies tailored to your specific situation.

These professionals can help you understand your pets' behaviors and suggest ways to improve interactions. They may also offer guidance on specific training techniques or help identify any underlying issues that need addressing.

Getting expert advice can make a significant difference in creating a peaceful multi-pet household. Sometimes, a little professional input can lead to a happier environment for everyone.

Caiques And Children Establishing Safe Boundaries

Caiques can make wonderful companions for children, bringing joy and excitement into the household. However, it's important to set safe boundaries to protect both the bird and your child. Here are some essential tips to help create a safe and happy environment for everyone.

1. Supervision is Key

The most important rule when it comes to caiques and children is supervision. Always keep an eye on interactions between your caique and your child. This ensures that both the child and the bird are safe and helps prevent any accidental harm.

Caiques are playful and curious, which can sometimes lead to unexpected situations. By supervising their interactions, you can intervene if things start to go wrong. For example, if a child accidentally scares the bird or tries to grab it, you can step in immediately to prevent any stress or injury.

Supervision also allows you to teach your child about the caique's behavior and needs. You can explain what the bird likes and dislikes, which helps children understand how to interact with it safely.

2. Teach Respect

It's essential to educate your children about how to interact with the caique. Teaching them to be gentle and calm will help ensure positive experiences for both the bird and your child. Explain to your kids that caiques can be easily frightened by loud noises or sudden movements.

Encourage your children to speak softly and approach the bird slowly. Show them how to offer their hand gently, allowing the caique to come to them rather than reaching out aggressively. This teaches respect for the bird's space and feelings, which is vital for building a trusting relationship.

You might also want to set an example by interacting with the caique in a calm manner. Children often learn by observing adults, so demonstrating gentle behavior can be very effective.

3. Set Rules

Establish clear rules about handling the caique. It's important for children to understand what is acceptable and what is not. For instance, children should never grab, chase, or corner the bird. Instead, they should be taught to let the bird come to them when it feels comfortable.

You can create a list of rules to remind your children of the proper behavior around the caique. Rules like "no loud noises," "don't poke or reach for the bird," and "let the bird come to you" can help them remember how to treat the caique respectfully.

Encourage your children to follow these rules consistently. You can even make it a fun game to remember the rules, rewarding them for good behavior with praise or small treats.

4. Create Safe Zones

Providing your caique with safe spaces is crucial for its well-being. Birds can become overwhelmed, especially in busy households with children. Make sure your caique has a quiet area where it can retreat if it feels stressed or anxious.

This safe space could be a specific room, a cozy corner, or even a covered area in its cage. Make sure this area is free from loud noises and chaos so the bird can relax and feel secure.

Teach your children to recognize when the caique needs some alone time. If the bird goes to its safe zone, remind your kids to give it space and not to disturb it. Respecting the bird's need for solitude will help maintain a peaceful environment for everyone.

5. Positive Experiences

Encouraging positive interactions between your caique and your children is essential for building a strong bond. One way to do this is by rewarding your children for gentle behavior around the bird.

When your child interacts calmly and respectfully with the caique, offer praise or small rewards. This reinforces good habits and helps them understand the importance of gentle behavior.

You can also encourage children to engage in positive activities with the caique, such as offering treats or playing with toys designed for birds. These activities can help your child learn to enjoy the bird's company while ensuring that the interaction remains positive and fun.

Taking Your Caique Out In Public

Taking your caique out in public can be a fun and exciting experience, both for you and your bird. However, it requires careful planning and attention to ensure that your caique feels safe and comfortable. Here are some tips to help make outings with your caique enjoyable and stress-free.

1. Use a Secure Carrier

When taking your caique outside, always transport it in a secure and well-ventilated carrier. This is the safest way to move your bird, as it prevents your caique from escaping or getting frightened by unfamiliar surroundings. A good carrier will have proper ventilation, enough space for your bird to move around, and a secure door that locks firmly.

Make sure the carrier is comfortable by adding a soft towel or blanket at the bottom. Your caique will feel more relaxed if the carrier feels cozy and familiar. Additionally, it's important to use the carrier at home occasionally, so your bird becomes accustomed to it before any public outings. This way, your caique will associate the carrier with a positive experience, rather than something stressful.

2. Choose Appropriate Locations

Not every place is suitable for taking a bird, so it's important to choose your outing locations carefully. Bird-friendly environments, such as parks or pet-friendly events, are great options for your caique to explore new sights and sounds. These environments allow your bird to experience nature while remaining safe.

Avoid places with loud noises, large crowds, or fast-moving animals, as these can overwhelm your caique. Public areas like shopping malls, restaurants, or busy streets are not the best places for birds, as they can cause stress and anxiety. Instead, start with calm and quiet places where your bird can feel more at ease.

Before going to any public space, check if they allow pets and whether it is a good environment for a small bird like your caique. This will help ensure a positive experience.

3. Limit Exposure

When taking your caique out for the first time, keep the outings short. New environments can be overwhelming for birds, especially when they're not used to being outside. Start with short trips, maybe 10 to 15 minutes, and gradually increase the time as your bird becomes more comfortable.

These short outings help your caique get used to new sights, sounds, and smells at a manageable pace. Over time, as your bird becomes more confident, you can take it on longer outings. Pay attention to how your caique reacts during these trips to gauge whether it's ready for more extended outings in the future.

4. Monitor Behavior

Your caique's behavior will tell you a lot about how it's feeling during an outing. Keep a close eye on your bird to watch for any signs of stress or discomfort. Signs of stress might include fluffing up feathers, excessive squawking, rapid breathing, or trying to hide.

If you notice your caique acting nervous or scared, it's important to either return home or find a quiet, calm place where your bird can relax. It's always better to cut an outing short if your bird seems uneasy, as this prevents your caique from becoming overwhelmed. You can always try again another day, gradually helping your bird adjust to outdoor experiences.

5. Bring Familiar Items

Bringing along familiar items can help your caique feel more secure in unfamiliar places. You can include favorite toys, blankets, or even perches in the carrier. These items provide comfort and reassurance to your caique, as they remind the bird of home.

Having familiar items in the carrier can make the new environment feel less scary. For example, a toy that your caique loves to play with at home can serve as a distraction, helping your bird relax during the outing. A favorite blanket can offer warmth and comfort, making the trip more enjoyable.

TRAVEL AND TRANSPORT

Traveling With Your Caique: Preparation And Tips

Traveling With Your Caique: Preparation And Tips

Traveling with your caique can be an enjoyable experience, but it requires careful planning to make sure your bird stays safe, comfortable, and stress-free. Caiques, like other birds, can become anxious or stressed when they are in a new environment, so it's important to prepare well before you hit the road.

Here are some simple and helpful tips to make traveling with your caique easier:

1. Get Your Caique Used to Their Carrier

Before you go anywhere with your caique, you need to help them feel comfortable in their travel carrier. Birds may feel anxious in unfamiliar spaces, so getting your caique used to the carrier beforehand will help ease their stress on the day of the trip.

To do this, you can place the travel carrier in their usual living space and leave the door open. Let your caique explore it on their own terms. You can even place some of their favorite toys, treats, or perches inside the carrier to make it feel more inviting. Doing this a few days or even weeks before your trip will give your bird time to get familiar with the carrier and see it as a safe space, not something to be afraid of.

2. Pack Essential Supplies

When traveling with your caique, you need to pack a travel kit with all the essentials. The most important things to bring are:

• Food: Pack enough of your bird's regular food to last the whole trip. Sudden changes in diet can upset their stomach or cause stress, so it's best to stick to what they usually eat.

• Water: Bring plenty of clean water for your bird. Traveling can dehydrate birds, especially in dry or warm conditions, so make sure your caique has access to water at all times.

• Medications: If your bird is on any medication, make sure to bring enough for the trip. You may also want to pack a small first-aid kit for your bird in case of emergencies.

• Toys and Perches: Bringing along your caique's favorite toys or perches can help them feel more at home during the trip. These familiar items will provide comfort and entertainment, which can reduce stress while on the road.

3. Plan Your Route and Stops

Whether you're traveling by car or plane, it's important to know the rules for transporting birds and plan your route accordingly.

- Car Travel: If you're driving with your caique, plan for regular stops along the way. Birds need breaks to stretch, eat, and drink water, so aim to stop every couple of hours. Make sure the car temperature is comfortable, as birds are very sensitive to heat and cold. Also, never leave your bird in a parked car unattended, as the temperature inside a car can rise or drop quickly.
- Air Travel: If you're flying with your bird, research the airline's rules and policies ahead of time. Some airlines allow birds in the cabin, while others may require them to be in the cargo hold. You may also need to provide certain documents, like a health certificate, from your vet. It's a good idea to call the airline in advance to clarify their requirements and make sure you have everything you need.

4. Check the Weather

The weather is an important factor when traveling with your caique. Birds are sensitive to temperature changes, so you'll want to avoid traveling during very hot or very cold weather.

- Hot Weather: In high temperatures, make sure your bird stays cool. Use air conditioning in the car, and never leave your bird in direct sunlight. Offer water often to prevent dehydration.
- Cold Weather: In cold temperatures, keep your bird warm by covering part of the carrier with a blanket. Make sure the blanket allows some airflow, so your caique still has fresh air. Also, check that the temperature in your car or plane is comfortable for your bird.

5. Stay Calm and Relaxed

Birds can pick up on your emotions, so try to stay calm and relaxed throughout the trip. If you're stressed, your caique might feel stressed too. Speak to your bird in a soothing voice, and give them plenty of attention to keep them calm.

Best Travel Cages And Carriers

When you travel with your caique, choosing the right travel cage or carrier is one of the most important things to consider. Your bird's comfort and safety depend on having a carrier that suits their needs, so it's essential to pick the right one. Here are some helpful tips on what to look for when selecting a travel cage or carrier for your caique.

1. Choose the Right Size

One of the first things to think about when buying a travel carrier for your caique is the size. The carrier needs to be big enough for your bird to stand up, move around a little, and stretch their wings slightly. However, it shouldn't be so big that your caique can get thrown around if you make a sudden stop or turn while traveling.

A good rule of thumb is to choose a carrier where your bird can stand comfortably on a perch, with enough space above their head so they don't bump into the top. At the same time, the carrier should not be too spacious, as a small, cozy space will help your bird feel more secure during the trip.

2. Pick a Sturdy Material

The material of the carrier is very important for your bird's safety. You want to choose a carrier made from strong, durable materials that can withstand bumps or impacts during travel.

Carriers made from stainless steel or heavy-duty plastic are often the best choices. These materials are sturdy enough to protect your caique and won't easily break or crack. Avoid carriers made from flimsy or lightweight materials, as these can be damaged easily, or worse, your bird might escape if the carrier gets broken during transport.

If you choose a plastic carrier, make sure it's made from thick, durable plastic, not thin or bendable materials. For metal cages, make sure the bars are strong and not too widely spaced, as your bird could get stuck or hurt if they try to squeeze through.

3. Ensure Good Ventilation

Your caique needs plenty of fresh air while traveling, so make sure the carrier has good ventilation. Look for carriers with lots of air holes or mesh panels that allow airflow without compromising safety.

Ventilation is especially important if you're traveling in warm weather or for long periods. A well-ventilated carrier will help keep your bird cool and comfortable, reducing the risk of overheating. However, make sure that the openings are not too big, as your bird could potentially escape or get injured if the gaps are wide enough for them to stick their head or wings through.

Mesh panels can be a good option for ventilation, but be sure they are made from sturdy material that your bird can't chew through. Caiques are known to be strong chewers, so weak mesh could be a problem if your bird decides to test it with their beak.

4. Focus on Security

When it comes to picking a travel carrier for your caique, security is key. Birds are clever creatures, and some, including caiques, can figure out how to open simple latches or locks. You'll want to choose a carrier that has a secure, reliable door lock to prevent your bird from escaping during the trip.

Look for carriers with strong locks or latches that are difficult for your bird to tamper with. Avoid carriers with simple twist locks or weak closures that your bird might figure out. Some carriers come with double-locking mechanisms or doors that lock securely into place, giving you peace of mind that your bird will stay safely inside.

Make sure the door itself is sturdy and closes tightly. During travel, your bird might try to push against the door, so it should be able to hold firm without opening.

5. Consider Additional Features

There are some extra features that can make a travel carrier even more convenient and comfortable for your bird. For example, some carriers come with removable trays for easy cleaning, which can be useful if your trip is long. Others may have built-in perches or areas to attach water and food dishes, which can make the trip more comfortable for your caique.

Handles or shoulder straps are also great additions that make it easier for you to carry the cage, especially if you'll be walking a lot or going through airports.

Reducing Stress During Travel

Traveling can be stressful for caiques because they are in a new environment and away from their usual routine. As birds are sensitive creatures, it's important to take steps to help them feel safe and calm during a trip.

Fortunately, there are some simple things you can do to make the experience more comfortable for your bird. Here are some tips to reduce your caique's anxiety while traveling.

1. Cover the Carrier

One of the easiest ways to help reduce your caique's stress during travel is to cover their carrier with a light cloth or blanket. By draping a cloth over the carrier, you block out some of the new sights and distractions that might make your bird anxious. When they can't see the busy environment outside, they're more likely to relax and feel secure.

However, it's important to make sure the cloth doesn't block the carrier's ventilation. Birds need a constant supply of fresh air, especially when traveling, so choose a lightweight fabric that allows air to flow through easily. Avoid covering the carrier completely—leave a small part open for airflow so your bird can breathe comfortably. You can also uncover the carrier a bit once your caique seems to be more relaxed or when you take a break during the trip.

2. Maintain a Routine

Caiques are creatures of habit, and sudden changes in their daily routine can make them feel uneasy. While traveling, it's helpful to keep their routine as close to normal as possible. Sticking to the same schedule for feeding, playtime, and rest will give your caique a sense of familiarity, even when they're in a new environment.

For example, if you usually feed your bird in the morning and evening, try to do the same while traveling. Bring along their favorite food and snacks, and give them meals at the same time you would at home. If your caique has regular playtime or gets out of the cage for exercise, try to incorporate that into the trip, even if it's just letting them out for a short time during rest stops.

By maintaining these small but important parts of their routine, you can help your caique feel more secure and less anxious, as they'll have something familiar to rely on during the journey.

3. Use Calming Aids

Another way to help ease your caique's stress during travel is by using natural calming aids. There are various products available, such as sprays, supplements, or calming drops, that are designed to help reduce anxiety in birds. These products often contain natural ingredients like chamomile, which can have a soothing effect on your bird.

Before using any calming product, it's important to talk to your vet. Not all products are safe for every bird, so your vet can recommend the best option for your caique and make sure it won't cause any harm. Some calming aids are sprayed inside the carrier, while others can be added to your bird's water or food. Make sure to follow the instructions carefully if you decide to use one of these products.

In addition to calming products, some owners play soft music or white noise to create a peaceful environment for their birds during the trip. This can help drown out loud or sudden noises that might startle your bird and create a more relaxing atmosphere inside the car or carrier.

4. Stay Calm and Reassuring

Your caique can pick up on your emotions, so it's important for you to stay calm and relaxed while traveling. If you're anxious or stressed, your bird might sense it and become more anxious as well. Try to talk to your bird in a calm, soothing voice throughout the trip, and give them plenty of attention to reassure them that everything is okay.

If you notice your bird becoming particularly stressed, give them a few minutes of quiet time. You can pause the trip and take a break to let your bird relax, check on their food and water, or simply sit quietly for a moment before continuing the journey.

5. Prepare for Stops

When traveling long distances, plan for regular rest stops to give your caique time to relax, eat, and drink water. Birds can become dehydrated or fatigued during travel, especially if the journey is long. Giving your bird time to rest and offering them a snack or drink at each stop will help keep them comfortable and reduce their stress.

During these breaks, you can also check your bird's carrier to make sure they are comfortable and that everything is in order. Sometimes just a little break is enough to calm an anxious bird and help them settle in for the rest of the trip.

CHAPTER 6

Vacation And Boarding Options For Caiques

If you're planning a vacation and can't take your caique with you, you'll need to make sure they're well cared for while you're away. Caiques are social, active birds, and it's important to ensure they receive proper attention and care even in your absence. Here are some great options for your bird's care while you're on vacation.

1. Hiring a Pet Sitter

One of the best options for your caique's care while you're away is hiring a professional pet sitter. A pet sitter can visit your home regularly, providing your bird with food, fresh water, and attention. This option is especially convenient because your caique can stay in their familiar environment, which helps reduce stress.

If you choose to hire a pet sitter, look for someone who has experience with birds, especially parrots. Caiques have specific needs, and not everyone knows how to handle birds properly. A pet sitter with bird-care experience will be able to interact with your caique confidently, clean their cage, and even play with them to keep them entertained.

Before hiring a sitter, it's a good idea to meet them and explain your bird's routine, feeding schedule, and preferences. Make sure they understand your bird's needs and are comfortable handling them. You might also want to provide the sitter with emergency contact information and the number of your vet, just in case.

2. Using a Boarding Facility

Another option for caring for your caique while you're on vacation is to use a boarding facility. Some boarding facilities specialize in birds and have the knowledge and equipment needed to take care of caiques. These facilities provide your bird with a safe, clean environment while you're away.

When choosing a boarding facility, it's important to do your research. Look for facilities with positive reviews and ask other bird owners for recommendations. Make sure to visit the facility in person before making a decision. During your visit, you can check the conditions, see how the staff interacts with the birds, and make sure the cages are clean and spacious.

A good bird boarding facility will offer personalized care, meaning they'll follow your instructions for feeding, cleaning, and interacting with your bird. They may also have vet services or access to a bird specialist in case of any health concerns. This can give you peace of mind, knowing your bird will be in good hands while you're away.

3. Trusted Friends or Family

If you have friends or family members who are familiar with birds, they may be able to take care of your caique while you're on vacation. This option can be a great choice if your bird already knows and is comfortable with the person taking care of them.

Having a trusted friend or family member care for your bird can be less stressful for your caique because they will be around someone they already recognize. Plus, your bird can stay in their own home if the person is willing to visit daily. You could also choose to bring your bird to their home, but make sure it's a safe environment for your caique, with no hazards like open windows, dangerous pets, or harmful objects.

Just like with a pet sitter, it's important to give your friend or family member clear instructions on how to care for your bird. Explain your caique's feeding schedule, how to clean their cage, and any other special needs they might have. It's also a good idea to leave emergency contact information and the name of your vet, just in case.

4. Things to Consider Before You Leave

Regardless of which option you choose, there are a few things you should do before you leave to ensure your caique's well-being:

• Stock up on supplies: Make sure you have enough food, water, and cleaning supplies for the entire time you'll be away. If you're boarding your bird or leaving them with someone, pack their favorite toys, food, and any treats they enjoy.

• Write detailed instructions: Leave a clear list of instructions for your pet sitter, boarding facility, or friend. This should include your bird's feeding schedule, cleaning routine, playtime needs, and any medical or behavioral notes they should be aware of.

• Emergency contacts: Leave your phone number, the name of your vet, and any other emergency contacts, so the person caring for your caique can reach out if anything happens.

• Prepare your bird for change: If possible, introduce your bird to the person who will be caring for them ahead of time. Let them interact with your bird so your caique feels more comfortable when the time comes. If you're using a boarding facility, visit the place with your bird a few times before your trip so they can get used to the new environment.

Taking Your Caique On Outdoor Adventures

Caiques are playful and energetic birds, and they may enjoy spending time outside. However, it's important to make sure your caique is safe while they explore the outdoors. Birds are fragile creatures, and the outdoor environment can be full of risks. If you want to take your caique on outdoor adventures, there are a few safety tips you need to follow to keep them protected.

1. Use a Bird Harness

One of the most important things to do when taking your caique outside is to use a bird harness. Never let your caique fly freely outdoors unless you are in a safe and enclosed space, such as a bird aviary. A bird harness is a special piece of equipment that fits around your caique's body and attaches to a leash. It allows your bird to move around and explore without the risk of flying away.

Caiques can get excited when they see the outdoors, and they may try to fly. If they aren't wearing a harness, they could get lost or hurt. Even if your bird's wings are clipped, they might still be able to fly short distances or catch a breeze, which can carry them away. A harness gives you control while still giving your caique the chance to experience the outdoors safely.

It's important to choose a harness that fits properly. It should be snug but not too tight, and it should allow your bird to move comfortably. Before taking your bird outside, get them used to wearing the harness indoors. This way, your caique will be more comfortable and less stressed when they go outside for the first time.

2. Monitor the Environment

When you're outdoors with your caique, always pay attention to your surroundings. The outdoor environment can be unpredictable, and there are several things that could pose a danger to your bird. For example, predators like hawks, eagles, or even cats may see your caique as prey. Always keep an eye on the sky and the ground to spot any potential threats. It's best to stay in open areas where you can see around you clearly.

Also, avoid taking your caique out in extreme weather. Birds are sensitive to both heat and cold, so try to choose mild, pleasant days for outdoor adventures. If it's too hot, your bird can overheat quickly, especially in direct sunlight. If it's too cold, your bird may become chilled, which can make them sick. Windy days can also be dangerous, as strong gusts can make your caique feel unstable or uncomfortable.

Bringing your bird outside in good weather conditions will make the experience more enjoyable for them and much safer overall.

3. Stay Close to Your Bird

Caiques are small birds with big personalities. They're curious and love to explore, which can sometimes get them into trouble. When you're outdoors with your caique, it's important to stay close and keep a close eye on them at all times.

Being outdoors exposes your caique to many new and unfamiliar things. They might try to chew on plants, leaves, or objects they find on the ground, which can be dangerous. Some plants and substances are toxic to birds, and there's also the risk of ingesting harmful bugs or bacteria. By staying near your caique, you can quickly stop them from putting anything harmful in their beak.

Additionally, caiques can move quickly and may try to explore areas they shouldn't, like under bushes, into small spaces, or near water. Always watch where your bird is going to prevent any accidents. You can allow your bird to walk and explore a little, but keeping them close will make sure they stay safe.

4. Provide a Comfortable Outdoor Experience

In addition to safety, it's important to make the outdoor experience comfortable for your caique. Bring along some familiar items, like one of their favorite perches or a toy, to help them feel more at ease. If you're planning to be outside for a while, make sure to bring water and offer it to your bird regularly to keep them hydrated.

    Pay attention to how your bird is behaving. If they seem nervous or stressed, it may be best to bring them back inside to their familiar environment. Not all birds enjoy the outdoors the same way, and some may take a little time to get used to it.

Chapter 7

BREEDING AND REPRODUCTION

Is Breeding Right For You?

Before deciding to breed caiques, it's important to carefully consider whether it's the right decision for you. Breeding birds is not as simple as allowing them to mate and waiting for chicks to hatch. It involves a lot of responsibility, effort, and resources. Here are some key points to think about before you begin.

1. Time Commitment

Breeding caiques can take up a lot of your time. From the moment you decide to breed them, you'll need to pay close attention to the birds throughout the entire process. During mating, egg-laying, and chick-rearing, there are many things that can go wrong, so it's essential to be present and ready to step in if needed.

For example, if the parents don't feed the chicks properly, you'll need to assist with feeding the babies yourself. Hand-feeding newborn chicks requires special skills, time, and effort. The feeding needs to happen multiple times a day, often at inconvenient hours like early in the morning or late at night. You will also need to monitor the health and development of the chicks closely to ensure they are growing as they should.

Breeding birds isn't a short-term project—it's a long-term commitment that could last several months or more, depending on how many chicks you have and how long it takes for them to become independent.

2. Space and Resources

Do you have enough space to care for a growing family of caiques? Caiques are active, energetic birds that need plenty of room to move around. If you breed them, you'll need to have adequate space for the parents and the chicks. Once the chicks are born, they will need to be housed in safe, comfortable cages with enough room for them to grow.

In addition to space, you'll also need the right equipment and supplies to care for the birds. This includes nesting boxes for the parents, special food for the chicks, toys, and perches to keep the birds entertained, and cleaning supplies to keep their environment clean and healthy. As the chicks grow, they will require larger cages or additional space. All of this can add up quickly, so it's important to be sure you have enough room and resources to handle breeding.

3. Financial Considerations

Breeding caiques can also be expensive. Raising healthy chicks requires more than just food and water. You'll need to invest in high-quality bird food, supplements to support the health of both the parents and the chicks, and possibly extra cages as the chicks grow.

Veterinary care is another important cost to consider. Birds, especially young chicks, may require visits to the vet to ensure they are healthy. If any health issues arise, the costs can increase quickly. Sometimes, unexpected problems like egg-binding (when a bird has trouble laying an egg) or illnesses in the chicks may require medical intervention, which can be expensive.

Make sure you are financially prepared for the potential costs before deciding to breed caiques. It's important to have a budget in place to cover food, supplies, and any vet bills that may come up.

4. Long-Term Responsibility

Breeding caiques is not just a short-term task—it comes with long-term responsibility. Once the chicks hatch and grow, it's your duty to ensure they are cared for properly, either by you or by finding suitable homes for them. Finding good homes can be difficult, as not everyone knows how to properly care for birds like caiques. You need to make sure the new owners understand the responsibility of owning a bird and are willing to provide a good, loving home.

If you cannot find homes for the chicks, you must be prepared to keep them yourself. This means more long-term space, time, and financial resources. Caiques are long-lived birds and can live for 20 years or more, so this is not a short-term responsibility.

5. Knowledge and Expertise

Breeding caiques requires more than just basic knowledge of bird care. You'll need to understand the mating process, how to care for eggs, and how to help raise chicks. If you're not familiar with breeding, it's important to do plenty of research or seek advice from experienced breeders before starting. Breeding birds without the right knowledge can result in poor health for the parents or chicks, and it can lead to mistakes that could be avoided with proper preparation.

Having access to a trusted avian vet who specializes in bird care is also important, as they can provide guidance and support throughout the breeding process. The vet can help monitor the health of the parents and chicks and assist with any problems that may arise.

Creating A Suitable Nesting Environment

Once you've decided to breed your caiques, the next important step is to create a comfortable and safe nesting environment for them. Caiques need the right space to lay their eggs and raise their chicks, and this involves setting up a proper nesting box, choosing suitable materials, and ensuring the right conditions in the environment. Let's go over how to create the perfect nesting setup for your caiques.

1. Choosing a Suitable Nesting Box

The most important part of the nesting environment is the nesting box. This is where your female caique will lay her eggs and where the chicks will grow. The nesting box needs to be the right size—big enough for both the male and female birds to move around comfortably, but not so large that it feels too open or unsafe for the birds.

A typical nesting box for caiques is about 12 inches long, 10 inches wide, and 12 inches high. This size provides enough room for the birds while also giving them a cozy space to feel secure. If the box is too big, the birds might not feel as protected, and if it's too small, they won't have enough space to move around and care for the eggs properly.

Make sure the nesting box has a secure entrance hole that the caiques can easily access, but one that isn't too large, as you don't want the chicks to accidentally fall out once they hatch.

2. Providing the Right Nesting Materials

Caiques like to build their nests with soft, comfortable materials. You'll need to provide them with nesting materials that they can use to create a soft bed for their eggs. The most common materials are wood shavings or shredded paper. It's important to make sure that whatever materials you use are clean, non-toxic, and free from dust. Dusty materials can irritate the birds' respiratory systems and cause health problems, so avoid anything that might harm them.

Wood shavings from untreated, bird-safe wood like aspen are a good choice because they are soft and easy for the birds to arrange. Avoid cedar or pine shavings, as these can release harmful fumes. If you prefer shredded paper, make sure it is free from ink or chemicals.

Once you've placed the materials in the nesting box, the caiques will likely start arranging it to their liking. They will create a comfortable and warm nest where the eggs can be safely laid and kept warm.

3. Choosing the Right Location for the Nesting Box

Where you place the nesting box in your caiques' cage is very important. The birds need to feel safe and secure when laying their eggs and caring for their chicks. If the nesting box is in a noisy or busy part of your home, the caiques may feel stressed or disturbed, which can affect their breeding and caring process.

The best place for the nesting box is in a quiet, calm part of the cage. Choose a location that is out of direct traffic flow, away from noisy areas like the TV or kitchen. This helps the birds feel more relaxed and focused on caring for their eggs and chicks.

Additionally, make sure the nesting box is securely attached to the cage. It shouldn't move or shift, as this could disturb the birds and make them feel less safe. A stable, secure nesting box will help the caiques feel more comfortable during the breeding process.

4. Controlling Temperature and Lighting

The environment around the nesting box needs to be warm and stable. Birds, especially breeding birds, are sensitive to temperature changes, so make sure the area isn't too hot or too cold. Keeping the temperature around 70 to 80 degrees Fahrenheit is usually comfortable for caiques during the breeding process.

If your home tends to be drafty, you may want to use a small heater or heat lamp nearby to maintain a stable temperature, but be careful not to place it too close to the birds. Overheating can be just as dangerous as cold temperatures.

Lighting is another important factor. Caiques need natural or soft lighting in their environment. Too much bright, direct sunlight can disturb the birds and make them feel uneasy, especially during breeding. It's best to provide indirect lighting or use a soft light source to keep the area comfortable. Natural daylight is ideal, but if you're using artificial lights, make sure they aren't too harsh.

If possible, set up the cage and nesting box in a room with natural light that follows the day-night cycle. Caiques will feel more in tune with their natural rhythms if they have access to this type of lighting.

5. Monitoring the Nesting Environment

Once everything is set up, continue to monitor the nesting environment to ensure that it stays safe and comfortable. Check the nesting materials regularly to make sure they're clean and dry, and replace them if they become soiled. Keep an eye on the temperature and lighting conditions as well.

During this time, it's important to give the birds some space and avoid handling them too much, especially when they're spending time in the nesting box. Caiques can become protective of their eggs, so it's best to let them focus on their task without too much interruption. However, make sure you're close enough to monitor their progress and step in if any problems arise.

Breeding Behavior And Mating Rituals

When caiques are ready to breed, they show specific behaviors and rituals that help them form bonds and prepare for mating. Understanding these behaviors will help you know when your birds are ready to mate and what to expect during the process. Breeding caiques is an exciting but delicate process, so paying close attention to their behaviors will ensure everything goes smoothly. Let's explore the key steps involved in caiques' breeding behavior and mating rituals.

1. Pair Bonding

One of the first signs that caiques are ready to breed is when they start forming a strong bond with each other. This bonding process is essential for successful breeding. You may notice that the male and female spend more time together than usual, grooming each other, feeding each other, and staying close.

Grooming, or "preening," is a way caiques show affection and strengthen their connection. If you see your caiques grooming each other frequently, this is a good sign that they are becoming a bonded pair. Feeding each other is another important behavior. The male may bring food to the female, offering it to her as part of the bonding process. These behaviors indicate that the birds are forming a trusting relationship, which is a key part of courtship before mating.

Pair bonding can happen over time, so it's important to give the birds space to build this relationship naturally. Once they have bonded, they are more likely to engage in mating behavior.

2. Mating Rituals

When caiques are ready to mate, they perform specific mating rituals. These rituals help the birds communicate their interest in each other and prepare for mating. The male caique usually initiates the mating process by displaying certain behaviors to attract the female.

One common display is the male spreading his wings wide and showing off his colorful feathers. This is done to impress the female and get her attention. The male may also bob his head up and down, which is another way of showing interest. During this time, the male might make special sounds, such as chirps or calls, to further communicate with the female.

If the female is interested, she will respond by allowing the male to approach her. The female may lower her body or turn slightly to show that she is ready for mating. This is a clear signal that she accepts the male's advances. If the female isn't ready, she might move away or ignore the male's displays.

Once both birds are comfortable with each other, mating will occur. This process can happen multiple times as the birds prepare for egg-laying. Keep in mind that it's important to give the birds privacy during this time. Avoid disturbing them, as they need to feel safe and secure to complete the mating process.

3. Egg-Laying Process

After successful mating, the female caique will begin the process of laying eggs. Caiques typically lay between 3 and 5 eggs, but this can vary. The eggs are not laid all at once. Instead, the female will lay one egg every 2 to 3 days until the full clutch (group of eggs) is complete.

During this period, it's important to provide the female with a comfortable, quiet nesting environment. As mentioned earlier, having a well-prepared nesting box with soft materials will give her a safe place to lay her eggs.

The female will spend most of her time in the nesting box during this phase, carefully laying and protecting the eggs. You might notice that the female becomes more protective and may not leave the nesting box often, as she will want to keep the eggs safe and warm.

4. Incubation Period

Once all the eggs have been laid, the incubation period begins. Incubation is when the female sits on the eggs to keep them warm and ensure they develop properly. For caiques, the incubation period usually lasts around 24 to 27 days. During this time, the female will stay in the nesting box most of the time, keeping the eggs warm with her body.

The male caique also plays an important role during this period. He will often bring food to the female, allowing her to stay on the eggs without needing to leave for long periods. This teamwork between the male and female helps ensure that the eggs are properly cared for.

It's important to keep the nesting environment quiet and stable during the incubation period. Any disturbances can stress the female, and it's crucial that she stays focused on keeping the eggs warm.

5. Hatching and Beyond

After about 24 to 27 days, the eggs will begin to hatch. Chicks usually hatch one by one, with a few days between each chick. This is because the eggs were laid on different days, so they won't all hatch at the same time.

Once the chicks start hatching, both the male and female caiques will work together to feed and care for them. The parents will provide food and warmth, helping the chicks grow strong and healthy. During this time, it's important to continue providing a stable, quiet environment for the birds to care for their young.

Caring For Eggs And Chicks

Once your caique eggs are laid, your role in their care is crucial. The period after egg-laying requires attention and understanding to ensure the eggs and chicks develop safely and healthily. Here's what you need to know about incubating the eggs, monitoring their condition, and caring for the chicks after they hatch.

1. Incubation of the Eggs

After the female caique lays her eggs, she will spend most of her time sitting on them to keep them warm. This process is called incubation. During this period, the female is very dedicated to her eggs. She will only leave the nest briefly to eat, drink, or take care of her hygiene. The male caique often helps during this time by bringing food to the female so she can stay on the eggs longer.

It's essential to ensure that both the male and female caiques have plenty of fresh food and water available during this time. Offer a balanced diet that includes seeds, fruits, and vegetables, as well as pellets designed for caiques. Providing a calm and quiet environment is also crucial. Loud noises or disturbances can stress the birds, which might affect their ability to incubate the eggs properly.

2. Monitoring the Eggs

Regularly checking on the eggs is an important part of the process. While you don't want to disturb the birds too much, it's essential to ensure that the eggs are healthy. You should look for any signs of problems, such as cracked eggs, dirty nesting materials, or the parents neglecting the eggs.

If you notice any cracked eggs, it may be necessary to remove them to prevent the parents from being stressed or confused. Similarly, if the parents seem uninterested in the eggs or are not providing adequate care, you may need to step in. In such cases, consulting a veterinarian who specializes in birds can provide guidance on how to handle the situation.

Eggs should not be moved unless absolutely necessary, as the parents need to be able to incubate them effectively. However, if you do need to handle the eggs, be sure to wash your hands thoroughly and handle them gently to avoid damaging them.

3. Caring for the Chicks

Once the eggs hatch, the fun really begins! The chicks will emerge one by one, usually within a few days of each other. After hatching, the parents will typically take over the care of the chicks. They will feed them by regurgitating food, providing the necessary nutrition for their growth.

It is important to monitor the chicks daily to ensure they are growing properly and receiving enough food from the parents. Look for signs that the chicks are active and alert. If you notice that the chicks are not getting enough food, or if they seem weak or sickly, you may need to intervene.

In such cases, you might have to hand-feed the chicks using a special bird formula. This formula is usually available at pet stores or through your veterinarian. Be sure to follow the instructions carefully and use the appropriate feeding tools, such as a syringe or a small spoon. Hand-feeding requires patience and gentle handling, so take your time and be careful not to overfeed or underfeed the chicks.

4. Feather Development

As the chicks grow, they will begin to develop feathers. This process usually starts within the first few weeks after hatching. You will notice that they go from being completely featherless to slowly getting their first feathers. It's essential to keep the chicks warm and clean during this period, as they are still very vulnerable.

You can help maintain a warm environment by ensuring that the nesting area is draft-free and at a comfortable temperature. If it gets too cool, the chicks may become stressed, which can lead to health issues. Providing a safe and clean nesting box will also help protect them from potential harm.

5. Watching for Behavior Changes

As the chicks grow and develop, you may notice changes in their behavior. They will start to become more active, exploring their environment and interacting with their parents more. This is a positive sign that they are healthy and thriving.

Make sure to provide the parents with plenty of food during this time, as they will be busy feeding the chicks. Continue to monitor the chicks closely, watching for signs of good health, such as normal weight gain and active behavior. If you see any concerning signs, such as lethargy or difficulty moving, consult a veterinarian who can provide advice.

Ethical Considerations And Responsibilities

Breeding caiques, or any other pets, comes with important ethical responsibilities. It's not just about producing chicks; it's about ensuring the well-being of all the birds involved and making thoughtful, responsible decisions throughout the process. Before deciding to breed caiques, it's essential to think carefully about why you want to breed them and to understand the long-term commitments that come with it.

1. Overpopulation: Be Mindful of Bird Overpopulation

One of the most important ethical issues to consider when breeding caiques is the risk of overpopulation. There are already many birds, including caiques, that need homes. Pet stores, breeders, and animal shelters often have birds looking for new owners. If you breed your caiques without thinking about what will happen to the chicks, you might contribute to this problem.

Before you start breeding, ask yourself if you have a plan for what will happen to the chicks. Can you take care of more birds yourself? Or do you have good, responsible homes lined up for them? Never breed birds just to make money or without thinking about their long-term care. It's crucial to have a clear, thoughtful plan in place before you begin breeding.

2. Health and Safety: Prioritize Your Birds' Well-being

The health and safety of your caiques should always be your top priority. Not all birds are fit for breeding, and it's important to make sure that both the male and female are in good health before allowing them to mate. Breeding birds that are sick or have genetic issues can result in weak or unhealthy chicks. These chicks may suffer from health problems later in life, and that's something you want to avoid.

To make sure your birds are healthy, take them for regular checkups at a vet who specializes in birds. A vet can confirm that your caiques are fit for breeding and help you spot any potential health issues early on. In addition, always keep your birds' living environment clean and provide them with a healthy diet full of essential nutrients.

If your caiques have any history of illness or genetic problems, it's best not to breed them. This helps ensure that you are not passing on health issues to future generations of birds. Breeding should always be done with the health and well-being of the birds in mind.

3. Finding Homes for the Chicks: Rehoming Responsibly

If you do decide to breed your caiques, another ethical responsibility is finding good homes for the chicks. If you plan to sell or rehome them, you need to make sure the people taking the birds are prepared and capable of caring for them. Caiques are not low-maintenance pets; they are energetic, intelligent, and need plenty of attention, stimulation, and proper care.

When selling or rehoming the chicks, take the time to screen potential buyers. Ask them questions about their experience with birds, their knowledge of caiques, and their ability to provide a good, permanent home for the bird. If someone doesn't seem ready for the responsibility of owning a caique, it's better to wait and find someone else who is more prepared. You want to make sure the chicks go to people who will love and care for them properly.

Additionally, it's a good idea to provide new owners with information on how to care for caiques. This can include details about their diet, behavior, housing needs, and social requirements. Helping new owners understand what to expect can improve the chances of a smooth transition for the chicks into their new homes.

4. Long-term Commitment: Being Ready for the Responsibility

Breeding birds isn't a short-term project; it comes with long-term responsibilities. If you breed your caiques, you need to be prepared for all outcomes, including the possibility that you won't be able to find homes for the chicks right away. If that happens, you will need to take care of the chicks until they find good homes, which could take weeks, months, or even longer.

This means you need to be ready to provide food, shelter, and attention to multiple birds for an extended period of time. It's also important to be aware that breeding caiques can sometimes result in complications, like chicks needing special care or attention. In these cases, you might have to hand-feed the chicks or take them to the vet for medical care, which can be time-consuming and expensive.

You also need to be aware that some chicks may not survive. This is a sad reality of breeding, and it's something you must be emotionally prepared for. It's essential to understand that not every breeding attempt will go perfectly, and being responsible means doing everything you can to ensure the health and safety of your birds while also being prepared for the unexpected.

CAIQUE LIFESPAN AND AGING

The Stages Of A Caique's Life

Caiques, like many other types of birds, go through different stages in their life as they grow and develop. Knowing what to expect at each stage can help you provide the right care and support for your bird, ensuring they stay healthy and happy throughout their life.

1. Baby Stage (Hatchling to Fledgling)

The baby stage of a caique's life begins as soon as they hatch from their egg. This period lasts until they are about three to four months old. During this time, caiques are completely dependent on their parents or caregivers for their needs. They rely on the adults to keep them warm and to provide food, which is usually regurgitated by the parents in the wild or hand-fed by caregivers in captivity.

At this stage, baby caiques don't have all their feathers yet, and their bodies are still very fragile. As they grow, they slowly develop their feathers and start learning important skills like flying. This is also the time when they begin to explore their surroundings a little, becoming more independent day by day.

Providing a safe and warm environment is essential during the baby stage. If you are hand-raising a baby caique, make sure to follow a strict feeding schedule with the right type of formula to ensure the baby gets the nutrients it needs.

2. Juvenile Stage (4 Months to 1 Year)

The juvenile stage starts around four months old and lasts until your caique is about one year old. This is a fun and exciting time because juvenile caiques are full of energy. They begin to explore the world around them more actively and start to show their playful and curious personalities. Caiques at this stage are known for being highly social, and they will spend a lot of time learning behaviors by interacting with their environment, toys, and people.

At this age, it's important to provide plenty of toys and activities to keep them entertained. Caiques are very intelligent birds, so mental stimulation is just as important as physical exercise. Social interaction with you or other birds is also key, as caiques are naturally very social creatures.

In the juvenile stage, caiques also learn social behaviors that will stay with them throughout their lives. This is the time to start training and teaching them good habits, such as how to interact nicely with people and other pets. Be patient and consistent, as they are still learning.

3. Adult Stage (1 to 10 Years)

Once your caique reaches its first birthday, it is considered an adult. The adult stage is typically the prime of their life, lasting from around 1 year old to about 10 years old. During this time, caiques are usually at their healthiest and most active. They have fully developed their personalities by now, and you will likely see a lot of the traits that caiques are known for, such as their playful nature, energy, and love for interaction.

As an adult, your caique will require a balanced diet that includes seeds, pellets, fruits, vegetables, and occasional treats. Exercise is also very important to keep them physically fit and prevent boredom. Make sure your bird has enough room to move around and stretch its wings, and continue to provide toys and activities that stimulate its mind.

This is also the best time for bonding with your caique, as they are highly social and enjoy spending time with their human companions. Regular interaction, training, and playtime are essential to keep them happy and engaged.

4. Senior Stage (10+ Years)

Caiques typically enter their senior years after the age of 10, although they can live for 25 to 30 years or more. As your bird gets older, you may start to notice some changes in their activity levels and overall health. Senior caiques tend to slow down a little and may not be as energetic as they were in their younger years.

At this stage, it's important to adjust their care to meet their changing needs. For example, you might need to make their cage more comfortable by adding extra perches or soft bedding. Senior caiques may also develop age-related health problems, so regular checkups with a vet who specializes in birds are essential. Keep an eye on their diet as well, ensuring they are eating enough nutritious food to support their health as they age.

While your caique may not be as active in its senior years, it will still enjoy spending time with you. Make sure to give it plenty of attention and continue offering toys and activities that are appropriate for an older bird. Keeping your senior caique mentally stimulated and comfortable will help ensure it remains happy and healthy in its later years.

Signs Of Aging In Caiques

As your caique parrot gets older, you may start noticing signs of aging. These changes happen gradually, so it's important to pay close attention to your bird's behavior and appearance. By being aware of these signs, you can adjust your care to keep your caique healthy and comfortable as they age.

Reduced Activity

One of the most noticeable signs of aging in caiques is a decrease in their activity level. Younger caiques are known for being very energetic and playful, but as they get older, they may slow down. Your older caique might spend more time sitting quietly in their cage or resting instead of playing or exploring. While it's normal for older birds to become less active, it's still important to provide them with opportunities for exercise. Gentle play and time out of the cage will help keep their muscles and joints healthy, even if they aren't as lively as before.

Changes in Feathers

As caiques age, you may notice changes in their feathers. The once bright and shiny feathers may lose their luster, appearing dull or worn. In some cases, older caiques might start plucking their feathers, which can be a sign of discomfort, stress, or illness. Feather plucking could also be related to skin issues or other health problems that become more common with age. If you notice feather changes or plucking, it's a good idea to consult with a vet to make sure there are no underlying health issues.

Weight Changes

Older caiques may also experience changes in their weight. Some birds might lose weight as they age due to a slower metabolism or decreased appetite. Others may gain weight because they are less active and still eating the same amount of food. Regularly monitoring your bird's weight is important to ensure they are maintaining a healthy balance. If you notice significant weight loss or gain, talk to your vet about adjusting their diet or routine to better suit their needs as they get older.

Decreased Appetite

As your caique ages, they might become less interested in food or more selective about what they eat. A reduced appetite is normal in older birds, but it's important to make sure they are still eating enough to stay healthy. You can try offering a variety of foods to keep their meals interesting, and make sure to include nutrient-rich options to support their health. If your bird seems to be eating significantly less or refusing food altogether, it could be a sign of illness, and a visit to the vet may be necessary.

Slower Movements

Older caiques may start moving more slowly than they used to. This could be due to age-related issues like arthritis or joint pain, which can make it harder for them to climb or perch. You may notice that your bird is less steady on their feet or that they have difficulty getting around the cage as easily as they once did. To make things easier for your aging caique, you can lower perches and make sure they have a comfortable place to rest. Providing soft surfaces for perching can also help alleviate joint pain.

Adjusting Care For Senior Caiques

As your caique parrot gets older, you will need to make some changes to their care to ensure they stay healthy and comfortable. Aging birds have different needs than younger ones, and by adjusting their diet, cage setup, and other aspects of their daily life, you can help them enjoy a good quality of life as they age. Here are some simple ways to adjust the care for your senior caique.

Adjusting Their Diet

A senior caique's diet may need to be adjusted as they age. Older birds often benefit from a diet that is lower in fat and higher in fiber to support their digestion and overall health. Too much fat can lead to weight gain, especially as your bird becomes less active, while more fiber can help with digestion, which may slow down as your caique gets older.

You may also notice that your older caique has trouble eating hard pellets or seeds, possibly due to dental issues or just general weakness. In that case, you can offer softer foods that are easier for them to eat. This could include soaked pellets or softer fruits and vegetables. Adding more fresh fruits and vegetables to their diet will also help them get the vitamins and nutrients they need to stay healthy. Make sure their meals are balanced, and try to offer a variety of food to keep their diet interesting.

Modifying Their Cage Setup

As your caique gets older, they may have a harder time moving around in their cage. To help them, you can make some simple changes to their cage setup. For example, if your bird is struggling to climb or perch as easily as they used to, you can lower the perches to make it easier for them to reach. Ladders can also help them move around without needing to fly or climb too much.

Adding soft padding to the cage floor is another good idea. This can help cushion any falls if your bird slips or has trouble perching. You can also add flat perches, which provide a more stable and comfortable place for your caique to rest. These changes can make a big difference in your bird's comfort and help them feel more secure in their cage as they age.

Regular Vet Visits

As your caique ages, it becomes even more important to schedule regular check-ups with an avian vet. Older birds are more likely to develop health problems, and regular visits to the vet can help catch any issues early. This gives you a better chance of treating them before they become serious.

Most veterinarians recommend at least one annual check-up for older birds, but for senior caiques, it may be a good idea to schedule semi-annual visits, meaning every six months. This way, the vet can monitor your bird's health more closely and make recommendations as needed to adjust their care. A vet can also check for any signs of arthritis, dental issues, or other problems that are more common in older birds.

Providing Mental Stimulation

Even though your senior caique may not be as physically active as they were when they were younger, they still need mental stimulation to stay happy and healthy. Keeping their mind engaged is important for preventing boredom and keeping their brain sharp as they age.

You can continue to offer toys and puzzles that challenge their problem-solving skills, but keep in mind that your older caique may prefer less physically demanding activities. For example, they might enjoy foraging toys that require them to think, but don't need too much energy to interact with. Rotating their toys regularly and providing new, interesting objects for them to explore will help keep them mentally stimulated.

Common Health Issues In Older Caiques

As caiques get older, they can face a variety of health problems that are more common in senior birds. Being aware of these issues and their symptoms is important, as it allows you to catch potential problems early and seek the right treatment. Here are some common health issues you might see in older caiques, along with signs to watch for.

Arthritis

One of the most common health problems in older caiques is arthritis. This condition affects the joints and can cause stiffness and pain. As a result, you may notice that your caique is less active than before. They might not want to climb as much or may struggle to get to their favorite perches. You might also see them sitting for longer periods or moving more slowly. If your bird seems to be in discomfort or avoids using certain joints, it's a good idea to consult with a vet. They can provide pain relief options and suggest ways to make your caique more comfortable.

Respiratory Issues

Older caiques can also develop respiratory problems. These issues can arise from exposure to dust, poor air quality, or mold in their environment. You should be vigilant for signs of respiratory distress in your bird. Common symptoms include wheezing, labored breathing, coughing, or sneezing. If you notice your caique breathing heavily or appearing to struggle for breath, it's essential to seek veterinary care right away. Maintaining a clean living environment and ensuring good air quality can help prevent respiratory problems in your older caique.

Kidney and Liver Problems

Another concern for senior caiques is the risk of kidney and liver issues. These organs play crucial roles in filtering waste and maintaining overall health. If your caique develops problems with their kidneys or liver, you may notice some specific signs. Changes in their droppings, such as a shift in color or consistency, can indicate health issues. Weight loss is another red flag, as is lethargy, where your bird seems less energetic and more sluggish than usual. Regular vet check-ups can help monitor these organs' health, and any concerning symptoms should be reported to a veterinarian for further evaluation and treatment.

Vision and Hearing Loss

As caiques age, they may experience vision and hearing loss, similar to what happens in humans. This decline can make it harder for them to navigate their environment. You might notice that your caique seems startled more often, as they may not see you approaching or may not hear you coming. If your bird appears to bump into things or has trouble finding food, it could be due to declining eyesight or hearing. You can help your caique adjust to these changes by keeping their environment consistent and minimizing sudden movements around them.

Preventive Care and Regular Check-Ups

While aging can bring health challenges, regular check-ups with an avian vet can help catch problems early. These visits are important for monitoring your caique's overall health, especially as they enter their senior years. Your vet can provide advice on diet, exercise, and any necessary treatments for age-related health issues.

Creating a Comfortable Environment

In addition to regular vet visits, creating a comfortable and safe environment for your older caique is essential. Ensure their cage is easy for them to navigate, with lower perches and soft bedding to help prevent falls. Keeping their living area clean and free from dust and mold can also reduce the risk of respiratory issues.

Providing Comfort For An Aging Parrot

As your caique gets older, it's important to focus on making their life as comfortable as possible. Aging birds often have different needs, so adjusting their environment and daily routine can help them feel secure and happy.

Here are some tips to ensure your senior caique lives comfortably in their golden years.

Keep Their Environment Calm

As caiques age, they may become more sensitive to their surroundings. Loud noises or sudden movements can startle them, leading to stress and anxiety. To create a peaceful environment, keep their living space calm and quiet. This might mean placing their cage in a less busy area of your home, away from loud appliances, music, or children playing. If your caique seems startled by noises, try to minimize disruptions by closing doors or using soft lighting. By creating a serene atmosphere, you can help your bird feel more relaxed and secure.

Offer Warmth

Older caiques can struggle to regulate their body temperature, which means they may feel cold more easily. It's important to keep their cage in a warm and draft-free area. You can achieve this by placing their cage away from windows, doors, or vents where cold air might enter. Additionally, you can provide extra warmth with a heat lamp or a heating pad designed specifically for birds. These devices can help ensure your caique stays warm and cozy, especially during colder months or in air-conditioned environments. Always monitor the temperature to ensure it is comfortable for your bird and never place heat sources too close to the cage.

Be Gentle with Handling

As your caique ages, they may not enjoy being handled as much as they did when they were younger. Their joints and muscles can become more fragile, making them more sensitive to touch. It's important to respect their boundaries and handle them gently. Observe their body language to see if they seem comfortable or if they prefer to be left alone. If they show signs of discomfort or resistance, give them space. When you do handle your bird, support their body properly and move slowly to avoid startling them. This gentle approach will help your caique feel safe and cared for.

Spend Quality Time Together

Even if your older caique isn't as playful or active as they once were, they still crave companionship and love. Spending quality time with your bird is essential for their emotional well-being. Simply sitting next to their cage and talking to them can provide comfort and reassurance. You can also engage in gentle activities, such as offering head scratches, which many caiques enjoy. If your caique prefers to remain in their cage, you can spend time nearby, allowing them to feel your presence without feeling pressured to interact. These moments of connection can strengthen your bond and help your bird feel loved and secure.

Create a Comfortable Cage Setup

In addition to these general tips, consider adjusting your caique's cage setup to accommodate their changing needs. You can lower the perches to make it easier for them to climb. Adding soft bedding or mats to the cage floor can provide cushioning in case of any slips or falls. Make sure their food and water dishes are easily accessible to prevent them from having to stretch or climb too much. The more comfortable and safe their environment is, the better they will feel.

Monitor Their Health

Keeping your aging caique comfortable also involves being aware of their health. Regular vet check-ups are essential for monitoring any age-related health issues. If you notice changes in their behavior, eating habits, or mobility, consult your veterinarian. They can provide guidance on how to best support your bird's health during their senior years.

8

Chapter 8

CAIQUE SAFETY AND HAZARDS

Common Household Dangers (Toxins, And Wires)

Caiques are playful and curious birds, but they can get into trouble if they encounter common household dangers. It's important to be aware of these hazards to keep your caique safe and healthy. Here are some of the most common dangers you should watch out for in your home.

Toxic Plants

Many houseplants can be harmful or even toxic to caiques. Some popular plants, like philodendrons, pothos, and lilies, can cause serious health issues if your bird chews on them or eats their leaves. Before bringing any new plants into your home, it's crucial to check if they are safe for your caique. If you already have plants that are not safe, consider moving them to a location where your bird cannot reach them. Keeping your living space bird-friendly is essential for your caique's well-being.

Chemicals

Household cleaning supplies, paints, and other chemicals can be very dangerous for birds. Many of these products contain toxic ingredients that can harm your caique if they breathe in the fumes or ingest them. Always store these chemicals in a locked cabinet, well out of your bird's reach. When using any cleaning products, make sure the area is well-ventilated. It's best to keep your caique in another room until the air is clear and free of any harmful chemicals. This practice will help ensure that your bird remains healthy and safe from toxins.

Wires and Cords

Caiques love to chew on things, which can be a problem when it comes to exposed wires and cords from electronics, chargers, and appliances. If your bird finds these wires, it could lead to serious injuries or even electrocution. To keep your caique safe, make sure all wires are hidden or covered. You can use cord protectors or tape to secure loose cords, preventing your bird from reaching them. Additionally, check your furniture for any dangling cords that your caique might be able to grab. By taking these precautions, you can help keep your bird safe from the dangers of chewing on wires.

Non-Stick Cookware

Many people use non-stick cookware in their kitchens, but it's important to know that these pots and pans can release toxic fumes when heated. If the cookware is overheated, it can produce gases that are harmful to birds. To keep your caique safe, ensure that your bird is in another room while you're cooking. Instead of using non-stick options, consider switching to safer materials like stainless steel or cast iron. These alternatives are not only better for your caique but are also durable and long-lasting for your cooking needs.

Air Fresheners and Scented Candles

While air fresheners and scented candles can make your home smell pleasant, many of these products can be harmful to birds. The chemicals and fragrances used in these items can cause respiratory issues and other health problems for caiques. If you want to freshen the air in your home, consider using natural methods instead. Opening windows to let in fresh air or using a fan to circulate the air are great alternatives. These methods are not only safer for your caique but also help maintain good air quality in your home.

Additional Precautions

In addition to the dangers mentioned above, it's important to keep other household items in mind. For example, small objects like rubber bands, paper clips, and other small items can be choking hazards. Always be vigilant about keeping your living space tidy and free from small items that your caique could swallow.

It's also a good idea to supervise your caique when they are out of their cage. By keeping an eye on them, you can prevent them from getting into dangerous situations. Regularly inspecting your home for potential hazards will help create a safer environment for your bird.

Pet-Proofing Your Home

Creating a safe environment for your caique is essential for its health and happiness. One of the best ways to do this is by pet-proofing your home. This process involves taking steps to eliminate potential dangers and ensuring your bird can play and explore safely. Here are some important steps you can follow to pet-proof your home for your caique.

1. Designate a Safe Area

The first step in pet-proofing your home is to create a designated safe area for your caique. This space should be free from hazards, allowing your bird to play and explore without worry. Choose a room or a corner of a room where you can control the environment. Remove any toxic plants, dangerous items, or anything that could potentially harm your bird.

Make sure the area is spacious enough for your caique to move around freely and has appropriate toys and perches. Avoid placing your caique near windows or areas where they could get into trouble. By setting up a safe area, you provide a secure place for your bird to enjoy its time outside the cage.

2. Secure Windows and Doors

Birds, including caiques, can easily fly out of open windows or doors. To prevent this, always ensure that windows and doors are closed or securely screened when your caique is out of its cage. If you like to let fresh air into your home, consider installing screens on windows that your bird may access. This way, you can keep the windows open while preventing your caique from escaping.

It's also a good idea to check that any sliding doors or screen doors are securely closed before allowing your bird to roam freely. Regularly inspect screens for any holes or damage, as these can create escape routes for your caique.

3. Remove Small Objects

Caiques are curious birds and love to explore their surroundings. However, this curiosity can lead them to pick up small objects that may pose choking hazards. Items like coins, buttons, rubber bands, paper clips, and small toys can easily be mistaken for toys by your caique. To keep your bird safe, remove any small objects from the areas where it plays.

Regularly clean and organize your living space to ensure no small items are lying around. This proactive approach will help reduce the risk of your caique ingesting something harmful or getting choked on an object. Always be vigilant and keep an eye out for anything that could potentially harm your bird.

4. Check Furniture

When pet-proofing your home, it's crucial to inspect your furniture for any gaps or spaces where your caique could get stuck. Birds can be curious and may try to squeeze into tight spots. Check the edges of couches, chairs, and shelves for any gaps that could pose a risk. Make sure there are no areas where your caique could fall or get trapped.

You might also want to consider covering sharp corners with padding or moving furniture away from walls to minimize potential hazards. Additionally, avoid placing your caique's play area near furniture with loose cushions or items that could easily fall and hurt your bird.

5. Monitor Other Pets

If you have other pets, such as dogs or cats, it's essential to supervise their interactions with your caique. Some animals may see birds as prey, which can put your caique in danger. Create a safe area for your caique where it cannot be reached by other pets.

When introducing your caique to other pets, always do so under close supervision. Keep dogs on a leash or in a separate room during introductions.

Teach other pets to be calm around your bird, and never leave them alone together until you are confident that they can coexist safely.

Handling Emergencies And Accidents

Even with careful precautions, accidents can happen, and knowing how to handle emergencies is essential for your caique's safety and well-being. Being prepared can make a big difference when facing a crisis. Here are some important steps you can take to ensure you are ready to handle emergencies and accidents involving your beloved bird.

1. Identify a Veterinarian

One of the first steps in preparing for emergencies is to find an avian veterinarian. This is a veterinarian who specializes in birds and knows how to provide the best care for your caique. Research local veterinary clinics and identify one that has experience with birds. Make sure to familiarize yourself with their location, hours of operation, and any emergency procedures they have in place. Having this information ready can save precious time if you ever need to rush your caique to the vet.

Consider visiting the vet for a routine checkup before an emergency arises. This allows you to establish a relationship with the veterinarian and ensures that they know your caique's health history. During this visit, you can also ask questions about what to do in case of an emergency.

2. Prepare a First Aid Kit

Another essential step is to prepare a bird-specific first aid kit. This kit should contain important items that may be needed in case of an emergency. Some key supplies to include are:

- Sterile gauze: For covering wounds and stopping bleeding.
- Bandages: To wrap injured areas and protect them from dirt.
- Scissors: To cut bandages or gauze as needed.
- Tweezers: Useful for removing splinters or debris.
- Antiseptic wipes: For cleaning wounds before applying a bandage.

Additionally, keep a list of contact information for your veterinarian and emergency numbers in the first aid kit. This way, you will have everything you need in one place, making it easier to respond quickly during an emergency.

3. Recognize Signs of Distress

It's important to be aware of the signs that your caique may be in trouble. Recognizing symptoms early can help you take the necessary action before a situation worsens. Some common signs that your caique may be in distress include:

• Difficulty breathing: Watch for rapid breathing or gasping for air.

• Excessive sneezing: Frequent sneezing may indicate respiratory issues.

• Limping: If your caique is favoring a leg or appears unable to put weight on it, there may be an injury.

• Sudden changes in behavior: If your bird becomes unusually quiet, lethargic, or aggressive, it could indicate a health issue.

If you notice any of these signs, do not hesitate to contact your veterinarian immediately. Early intervention can often make a significant difference in the outcome of a health issue.

4. Knowing What to Do in an Accident

If your caique experiences an accident, such as a fall or injury, it's important to stay calm. Your calmness can help reassure your bird, which may be frightened or in pain. Begin by assessing the situation. Determine whether your caique needs immediate medical attention. If your bird is bleeding, take action right away. Use a clean cloth to apply gentle pressure to the wound to help stop the bleeding while you arrange to get to the vet.

If your caique seems alert but has a minor injury, observe it closely for any signs of distress or pain. If the injury does not improve or if your bird shows concerning symptoms, seek veterinary care as soon as possible.

5. Handling Toxic Exposure

Toxic exposure can happen if your caique ingests something harmful, such as a toxic plant or a household chemical. If you suspect that your bird has ingested a toxic substance, contact your veterinarian immediately. Time is critical in these situations. If possible, bring a sample of the substance with you to the vet. This will help the veterinarian understand what they are dealing with and provide the best treatment for your caique.

Predators And Outdoor Safety

Caiques are small and vulnerable birds, which makes outdoor safety extremely important. They can easily become targets for predators such as hawks, cats, and other animals. If you want to take your caique outside, there are several important steps you should follow to keep your bird safe and happy. Here's how to ensure your caique has a secure and enjoyable outdoor experience.

1. Supervised Outdoor Time

When taking your caique outside, it is essential to supervise them closely at all times. Birds can easily get frightened and fly away, which can lead to them getting lost or injured. To prevent this from happening, consider using a bird harness. A harness is a safe way to allow your caique to explore the outdoors without the risk of flying away.

When using a harness, make sure it fits properly and is comfortable for your bird. This will help them feel secure while they are outside. Once your caique is harnessed, you can take them to a safe area where they can enjoy fresh air and sunshine. Make sure to choose a quiet spot away from loud noises and busy areas, as sudden sounds can startle your bird.

2. Safe Enclosure

Another option for giving your caique outdoor time is to use a safe enclosure. You can either build or purchase a secure outdoor aviary specifically designed for birds. An aviary allows your caique to enjoy the outdoors while keeping them protected from potential predators.

When choosing or building an aviary, make sure it is sturdy and secure. It should have strong materials that cannot be easily broken or bent. The enclosure should also have a roof to prevent aerial predators like hawks from swooping down.

Inside the aviary, provide perches, toys, and other enrichment items to keep your caique entertained. This way, they can explore and play in a safe environment. An outdoor aviary is a great way for your bird to get fresh air, sunshine, and exercise without the risks associated with being outside unsupervised.

3. Awareness of Surroundings

Being aware of your surroundings is crucial when taking your caique outdoors. Always keep an eye out for potential dangers in the area. Birds of prey, such as hawks or eagles, can pose a serious threat to small birds like caiques. Watch for these birds circling overhead, as they may see your caique as potential prey.

To minimize the risk, avoid taking your bird out during times when predators are more active. Early mornings and late afternoons are times when many predators are hunting. Instead, try to take your caique outside during the middle of the day when predators are less likely to be around.

In addition to watching for birds of prey, be cautious of other animals. Cats, dogs, and wild animals can also pose threats to your caique. Always keep your bird in your sight and maintain control of the situation. If you see any animals approaching, take your caique inside or secure them in the aviary until the threat has passed.

4. Avoiding Stress

While enjoying outdoor time with your caique, it's essential to ensure that the experience is stress-free for them. New environments can be overwhelming for birds, so gradually introduce them to the outdoor setting. Start by spending short periods outside and increase the time as your caique becomes more comfortable.

Be mindful of loud noises, strong winds, and other environmental factors that may cause stress. If your caique appears frightened or anxious, it's best to take them back inside until they feel more at ease. Always prioritize their comfort and well-being during outdoor activities.

5. Providing Water and Shade

When your caique is outside, make sure to provide fresh water and shade. Birds can easily become overheated, especially in direct sunlight. Set up a shaded area for your caique to retreat to when they need a break from the sun.

Having fresh water available is also crucial. Offer a shallow dish of water that your caique can easily access. This will keep them hydrated while they enjoy their time outdoors.

CHAPTER 8

Seasonal Safety Tips (Winter, Summer Hazards)

Each season brings its own set of safety challenges for your caique. Being aware of these challenges and taking the right steps can help ensure your bird stays safe and healthy all year round. Here are some important safety tips for both winter and summer to keep your caique comfortable and secure.

Winter Safety Tips

1. Temperature Control

Caiques, like many birds, are sensitive to cold temperatures. During the winter months, it is important to make sure your home is warm enough for your caique. Birds can easily become chilled, so avoid placing their cage near drafts or cold windows.

To help keep your caique warm, consider using a space heater or a heat lamp in the room where their cage is located. Make sure that the heater or lamp is safe for use around birds, as some heating devices can be hazardous. Always monitor the temperature and ensure it remains comfortable, ideally between 65°F and 80°F (18°C to 27°C).

2. Humidity Levels

Winter air can often be very dry, which can harm your caique's respiratory health. Dry air can lead to problems such as dry skin, feather issues, and respiratory infections. To maintain healthy humidity levels, consider using a humidifier in the room where your caique is kept. This will help add moisture to the air, making it more comfortable for your bird.

If you don't have a humidifier, you can place a shallow dish of water near their cage. The water will evaporate and help increase humidity levels. Additionally, consider misting your caique lightly with water a few times a week to keep their feathers in good condition and to provide some moisture for their skin and respiratory system.

Summer Safety Tips

1. Avoid Overheating

Hot weather can be dangerous for your caique. Birds can easily overheat, which can lead to serious health issues. To prevent overheating during the summer months, ensure that your caique has access to cool areas in your home. Keep their cage in a shaded spot, away from direct sunlight.

Make sure to provide fresh water at all times, especially on hot days. Consider adding ice cubes to their water dish to help keep it cool. You can also use fans to help circulate air around their cage, but be sure they are positioned safely, away from where your caique can reach them.

Be aware of the signs of overheating in your caique, which can include excessive panting, fluffed feathers, and lethargy. If you notice any of these signs, immediately move your bird to a cooler area and offer water.

2. Bug Sprays and Chemicals

During the summer, many people use insecticides or other chemicals to keep pests away. These chemicals can be harmful to your caique, so it's crucial to take precautions. If you plan to use any insect sprays or chemicals, make sure your caique is in a different room. This will help prevent them from breathing in any harmful fumes.

After you use any chemicals, wait until the area is well-ventilated before allowing your bird to return. Open windows and use fans to help circulate air and remove any lingering odors or toxins. Always read the labels on products to ensure they are safe for use around birds.

EMOTIONAL WELL-BEING OF YOUR CAIQUE

Preventing Boredom And Loneliness

Caiques are playful and curious birds. To keep them happy and mentally stimulated, it's important to prevent boredom and loneliness. A happy caique is an active caique, and there are several ways to ensure your bird stays entertained and engaged. Here are some helpful tips to keep your caique feeling content and connected.

1. Toys and Activities

One of the best ways to keep your caique entertained is by providing a variety of toys. Caiques love to explore and play, so having different types of toys can keep their minds active and engaged. Here are some types of toys you might consider:

- Chew Toys: These toys allow caiques to chew and gnaw, which is natural behavior for them. They enjoy toys made from safe wood or soft materials that they can shred.
- Puzzles: Puzzle toys challenge your caique to think and solve problems. These toys often have hidden treats inside that your bird must figure out how to access.
- Foraging Toys: Foraging toys encourage your caique to search for food, mimicking their natural behavior in the wild. These toys can keep them busy and entertained for long periods.

Make sure to rotate the toys regularly to keep your caique interested. Introducing new toys and taking away old ones will make playtime exciting again. Interactive toys that require problem-solving skills can provide mental stimulation, which is important for your bird's overall well-being.

2. Social Interaction

Caiques are social creatures that thrive on interaction. They need time with their human companions to feel secure and happy. Here are some ideas for engaging with your caique:

- Daily Playtime: Spend quality time with your bird every day. You can talk to them, sing songs, or just sit and enjoy their company. Caiques love to be included in daily activities and will appreciate your attention.
- Play Games: You can also play games with your caique. Simple games like hide and seek, fetch with small balls, or even teaching them to catch can be fun for both of you. These interactions not only provide entertainment but also strengthen your bond.
- Offering Treats: Give your caique treats during your interactions. This could be their favorite fruits or special bird-safe snacks. Treats can be a great way to encourage them to come to you and engage with you.

If you have more than one caique, they can keep each other company and play together. Having a friend can reduce loneliness and provide entertainment when you are busy.

3. Training and Tricks

Teaching your caique new tricks or commands is a fantastic way to engage their minds. Training sessions can be fun and rewarding for both you and your bird. Here are some tips for effective training:

• Positive Reinforcement: Use positive reinforcement techniques, such as treats and praise, to encourage your caique. Whenever they perform a trick or follow a command, reward them immediately. This will help them associate good behavior with positive outcomes.

• Short Sessions: Keep training sessions short and fun, about 5 to 10 minutes. Caiques have short attention spans, so frequent short sessions will keep them interested and engaged.

• Learning New Skills: Teach them simple commands like "step up" or "spin" and gradually progress to more complex tricks. This will not only stimulate their minds but also create a stronger bond between you and your bird.

4. Outdoor Time

If possible, allow your caique to spend some time outside in a secure environment. Outdoor time can be a wonderful way for them to experience new sights and sounds. Here's how to make outdoor time safe and enjoyable:

• Secure Environment: Always supervise your caique closely while they are outside. Consider using a bird harness or a secure aviary to keep them safe from potential predators and other dangers.

• Fresh Air and Sunshine: Fresh air and natural sunlight are beneficial for your caique's health. Just make sure they have access to shaded areas to escape the heat if needed.

• Natural Exploration: Let your caique explore natural surroundings, such as trees and plants, safely. This can stimulate their senses and provide a rich experience that enhances their quality of life.

Managing Stress And Anxiety

Caiques, like all birds, can experience stress and anxiety, which can negatively affect their health and happiness. As a responsible pet owner, it's important to recognize the signs of stress and take steps to manage it effectively. By creating a calm environment and providing comfort, you can help your caique feel safe and secure. Here are some tips for managing stress and anxiety in your caique.

1. Identify Stress Triggers

The first step in managing stress is to identify what may be causing it. Every caique is different, and certain situations may stress one bird more than another. Common stress triggers for caiques can include:

• Loud Noises: Sudden loud sounds, such as thunderstorms, vacuum cleaners, or fireworks, can startle your caique and cause anxiety.

• Changes in the Environment: Moving furniture, changing the layout of their cage, or introducing new items can unsettle your bird.

• Unfamiliar Pets or People: New pets or visitors in the home can make your caique feel threatened or uncomfortable.

To identify stress triggers, observe your caique closely. Take note of any situations that seem to upset them or cause changes in their behavior, such as excessive feather plucking, vocalizations, or hiding. Once you know what causes stress, you can take steps to minimize those triggers in their environment.

2. Create a Safe Space

Providing a safe and quiet area where your caique can retreat when feeling stressed is crucial. This safe space can help them feel secure and calm. Here's how to create a comforting environment for your bird:

• Cozy Corner: You can designate a cozy corner of their cage as a safe retreat. Add soft bedding or blankets that they can snuggle into.

• Separate Room: If possible, consider having a separate room where your caique can go when they need a break from noise and commotion. This could be a quiet room away from bustling family activities.

• Hideaway Options: You can also include hideaway options within their cage, such as small boxes or covered perches, where they can go to feel safe and protected.

When your caique feels stressed, encourage them to go to their safe space. This area will serve as a comforting retreat where they can relax and regain their calm.

3. Establish a Consistent Routine

Caiques thrive on routine and predictability. Establishing a consistent daily schedule can help your bird feel more secure and reduce anxiety. Here are some ways to create a stable routine:

• Regular Feeding Times: Feed your caique at the same times each day. This helps them know when to expect food and can reduce anxiety about when their next meal will be.

• Scheduled Playtime: Set aside specific times for play and interaction each day. This can include training sessions, play with toys, or simply spending time together. Having regular playtime can be very reassuring for your caique.

• Predictable Interactions: Try to interact with your caique in the same way each day. This consistency helps build trust and makes them feel more secure.

By creating a structured routine, your caique will feel a sense of stability, which can significantly reduce feelings of anxiety and stress.

4. Gentle Handling

When handling your caique, it is essential to be gentle and calm. Birds can sense our emotions, so if you are nervous or rushed, they may become anxious as well. Here are some tips for gentle handling:

• Take Your Time: If your caique seems nervous, give them time to adjust to your presence before trying to hold them. Let them come to you on their own terms.

• Calm Environment: When you interact with your bird, try to create a calm environment. Speak softly and move slowly to avoid startling them.

• Comforting Touch: When you do hold your caique, use a gentle touch. Support their body properly and avoid sudden movements that may frighten them.

Building confidence takes time, so be patient with your caique. As they become more comfortable with your handling, they will feel more secure and relaxed.

Dealing With Separation Anxiety

Caiques are social birds that can become very attached to their owners. While this bond is wonderful, it can lead to separation anxiety when you leave them alone. Understanding how to manage this anxiety is important for your caique's well-being. Here are some effective strategies to help reduce their stress levels when you're not home.

1. Gradual Desensitization

One of the best ways to help your caique adjust to being alone is through gradual desensitization. This means slowly getting your bird used to the idea of you being away. Here's how to do it:

• Start Small: Begin by leaving your caique alone for just a few minutes. This could be as short as 5 minutes. When you leave, stay calm and don't make a big fuss. Just say goodbye and go.

• Increase Duration: Once your caique seems comfortable with short absences, gradually increase the time you are away. You might go to another room or step outside for 10 minutes, then 15, and so on.

• Return on Time: It's important to always return to your caique when you say you will. This teaches them that you will come back. If they learn that you always return, they will feel more secure when you leave.

• Be Patient: Every caique is different, so some may take longer to adjust than others. Be patient and go at your bird's pace. This gradual approach helps them build confidence in being alone.

2. Provide Distractions

Before leaving your caique alone, make sure to provide them with engaging distractions. Keeping their mind busy can help take their focus off your absence. Here are some ideas:

• Engaging Toys: Provide a variety of toys that your caique can play with. Chew toys, puzzle toys, and foraging toys are great options. These toys can keep them entertained and mentally stimulated.

• Foraging Activities: Create foraging opportunities by hiding treats in different places around their cage or in special foraging toys. This encourages natural behavior and keeps them busy searching for their food.

• Interactive Items: Rotate toys regularly to keep their interest. Introducing new toys can make playtime exciting and help reduce feelings of boredom and loneliness.

• Special Treats: Leave a special treat or two that they only get when you are away. This can make the time alone feel more like a special occasion.

3. Use Comfort Items

Sometimes, a familiar item can provide comfort to your caique when you are away. Here's how to use comfort items effectively:

• Personal Items: Consider leaving an item with your scent in their cage. This could be an old t-shirt or a piece of cloth you've worn. Your scent can be reassuring and make them feel more secure while you are gone.

• Favorite Toy: If your caique has a favorite toy or blanket, leave that with them. Familiar items can help them feel safe and reduce anxiety during your absence.

• Cage Setup: Ensure their cage is a comfortable and cozy environment. Adding soft bedding or a covered perch can provide a safe place for them to retreat to when they feel anxious.

4. Consider a Companion

If you find that you are often away from home and can provide adequate care, consider getting a second caique. Having a companion can be beneficial for your bird in several ways:

• Social Interaction: A second caique can provide companionship and play opportunities. They can entertain each other, which can help alleviate feelings of loneliness.

• Reduced Anxiety: Having a buddy can reduce separation anxiety. Your caique will feel more secure knowing they are not alone, and they can engage in social behaviors with their new friend.

• Shared Activities: Caiques can engage in play and foraging together, which can keep both birds mentally stimulated and happy.

Creating A Positive Living Environment

Creating a positive living environment is very important for your caique's emotional health and happiness. A well-thought-out space can help your bird feel safe, secure, and stimulated. Here are some steps you can take to enhance your caique's home life and ensure they thrive in their environment.

1. Cage Setup

The first step in creating a positive environment is to set up your caique's cage properly. A well-organized cage can make a big difference in their daily life. Here's what to consider:

• Spacious Cage: Make sure the cage is big enough for your caique to move around comfortably. They should have space to stretch their wings and explore. A larger cage allows for more toys and activities, which keeps your bird active and happy.

• Safe Environment: Ensure that the cage is safe and secure. Check for any sharp edges or small spaces where your caique might get stuck. The bars of the cage should be spaced closely enough to prevent your bird from escaping or getting their head stuck.

• Variety of Perches: Include different types of perches in the cage. Perches can be made of natural wood, rope, or even plastic. Having various sizes and textures encourages your caique to move around and exercise their feet.

• Food and Water Dishes: Provide separate dishes for food and fresh water. Make sure these are easily accessible and placed in a way that prevents them from getting dirty. Clean and refill these dishes regularly to ensure your caique stays healthy.

2. Environmental Enrichment

Caiques are playful and curious birds that need stimulation to keep their minds active. Environmental enrichment is key to preventing boredom. Here are some ideas:

• Change the Setup: Regularly rearrange the toys and perches in the cage. This change creates new challenges and keeps your caique interested. They love to explore, so a new layout can be exciting for them.

• Diverse Materials: Introduce various materials into the cage, such as branches, ropes, swings, and climbing toys. Natural branches can mimic the wild and provide a more enriching environment. Be sure to choose safe materials for your caique to chew on.

• Interactive Toys: Provide toys that encourage foraging and problem-solving. Toys that dispense treats or require the bird to figure out how to get to a reward can be especially engaging.

• Rotate Toys: Change toys regularly to keep things fresh. If your caique becomes bored with their toys, they may lose interest. Rotating toys allows your bird to rediscover old favorites and keeps their environment exciting.

3. Positive Interactions

Building a positive relationship with your caique is essential for their emotional well-being. Here are some tips for encouraging positive interactions:

• Gentle Communication: Speak softly to your caique and use a calm, soothing voice. Gentle communication helps build trust. Your caique will feel more comfortable when they hear familiar, friendly sounds.

• Body Language: Use gentle body language when interacting with your bird. Avoid sudden movements that might startle them. Slow, deliberate actions create a sense of safety, allowing your caique to feel more at ease.

• Spend Quality Time: Spend time with your caique every day. Play with them, offer treats, and engage in activities they enjoy. This regular interaction strengthens your bond and helps your caique feel loved and secure.

• Learn Their Preferences: Pay attention to what your caique enjoys. Whether it's a particular game, a favorite toy, or a type of treat, understanding their preferences can make your interactions more enjoyable.

4. Routine Care

Routine care is vital for maintaining a positive living environment. Keeping a clean and healthy space contributes to your caique's overall well-being. Here are some care tips:

• Regular Cleaning: Clean the cage regularly to prevent the buildup of waste, food, and debris. A clean environment is essential for your bird's health and can help prevent stress and illness.

• Change Food and Water: Make sure to change your caique's food and water daily. Fresh food and clean water are crucial for their health. Ensure that their dishes are clean to prevent any contamination.

• Observe Health: Regular care routines allow you to observe your caique closely. This way, you can notice any changes in behavior or signs of illness. Early detection can make a big difference in your bird's health.

• Provide Fresh Foods: Along with pellets or seeds, offer fresh fruits and vegetables. Variety in their diet can enhance their health and happiness.

CHAPTER 8

Recognizing Emotional Changes In Your Caique

Understanding your caique's emotional state is very important for their overall well-being. Like people, birds can experience a wide range of emotions, and being aware of changes in your caique's behavior can help you spot potential problems early. Here's how to recognize these emotional changes and what steps to take if you notice anything unusual.

1. Behavioral Changes

One of the first signs that something may be bothering your caique is a change in their behavior. Pay close attention to how your bird acts. Here are some specific behavioral changes to watch for:

• Withdrawal: If your caique suddenly becomes less active or spends more time alone, it could be a sign of emotional distress. They might stop playing with toys, interacting with you, or exploring their environment.

• Aggression: If your caique, who is usually friendly, starts to show aggressive behaviors, this may indicate that they are feeling threatened or anxious. Signs of aggression can include biting, lunging, or loud squawking.

• Decreased Activity: A drop in energy levels can also be a red flag. If your caique seems lethargic or uninterested in playing, it may be worth investigating further.

• Increased Vocalizations: On the other hand, if your caique suddenly becomes more vocal or noisy, this can be a sign of stress. They may be trying to express their discomfort or seek attention.

2. Physical Signs

In addition to changes in behavior, physical signs can also indicate that your caique is not emotionally well. Watch for the following:

• Feather Plucking: If your caique starts to pluck their feathers excessively, this could be a sign of anxiety or stress. Feather plucking can lead to bald spots and skin irritation.

• Over-Grooming: Similar to feather plucking, over-grooming can also indicate emotional issues. If your caique spends too much time grooming themselves, it may be a way to cope with stress or boredom.

• Changes in Appetite: If your caique suddenly eats less or refuses to eat, it can be a sign that they are feeling unwell or stressed. Conversely, overeating can also be a sign of anxiety.

• Physical Changes: Keep an eye out for any other physical changes, such as weight loss or changes in droppings. These can indicate health issues that may be linked to emotional distress.

3. Mood Swings

Caiques can experience mood swings, much like humans do. If you notice sudden changes in your bird's mood, it's essential to consider potential triggers. Here are some examples:

• Fearfulness: If your caique becomes suddenly fearful or skittish, think about what might have changed in their environment. New noises, unfamiliar people, or other pets in the home can cause anxiety.

• Aggression: Similarly, if your bird who usually enjoys being handled suddenly becomes aggressive, it could be due to stressors in their environment. Try to identify what might be causing this shift in mood.

• Curiosity: Sometimes, an increase in curiosity and playful behavior can indicate that your caique is feeling more secure and confident. Positive changes in their environment, such as new toys or interactions, can encourage this behavior.

4. Consulting a Professional

If you notice persistent changes in your caique's behavior or emotional state, it is essential to seek professional help. Consulting with an avian veterinarian or a bird behaviorist can provide valuable insights into your caique's well-being. Here's what you can do:

• Seek Expertise: A veterinarian who specializes in birds can help identify any underlying health issues that may be affecting your caique's behavior. They can also suggest treatments if needed.

• Behavioral Consultation: A bird behaviorist can provide strategies to improve your caique's emotional well-being. They can help you understand your bird's behavior better and offer advice on creating a more supportive environment.

• Monitor Progress: If you implement changes based on professional advice, keep track of your caique's behavior. Note any improvements or ongoing issues, and share this information during follow-up visits.

Made in the USA
Columbia, SC
13 March 2025